WITHDRAWN

THE IMPROBABLE SURVIVOR

STEVAN K. PAVLOWITCH

The Improbable
Survivor

Yugoslavia and its Problems

1918-1988

OHIO STATE UNIVERSITY PRESS
COLUMBUS

Published in the United States of America
by Ohio State University Press,
Columbus, Ohio 43210
Printed in England on long-life paper

Library of Congress Cataloging-in-Publication Data
Pavlowitch, Stevan.
The improbable survivor: Yugoslavia and its problems, 1918–1988/
Stevan Pavlowitch.
p. cm.
Bibliography: p.
Includes index.
ISBN 0–8142–9486–4
1. Yugoslavia—History—1918–1945.   2. Yugoslavia—History—1945–
I. Title.
DR1282.P38 1988   88–25334
949.7'02—dc19   CIP

Za Kostu

PREFACE

'For the time being, Yugoslavia exists by some sort of a miracle,' a well-known Yugoslav writer told me when we discussed this book. 'But you, as a historian, will recognize that miracles are facts of history – not to be underestimated.'

Yugoslavia was born on 1 December 1918. The anniversary has not been observed since the war, for the Unification Day of the 'First Yugoslavia', seen as flawed by some invalidating defect, has been brought forward by a couple of days, to 29 November (1943, the Jajce Declaration of the Anti-Fascist Council, and 1945, the proclamation of the Federative People's Republic), when better foundations are said to have been secured for a 'Second Yugoslavia'. In fact, both 1918 and 1943–5 were defective, Yugoslavia has been going on for seven decades, and many people in the country are now talking of a transition to a 'Third' one.

Paradoxically, Yugoslavia is still being denied its history, and yet it lives in the past. The Communist regime, like its monarchical predecessor, but so much more intensely and for so much longer, has kept to the heroic rendering of events. It is dangerous to try and shut away the past, to rewrite history, and fix it, for it always wriggles out of place and returns, often distorted. The study of Yugoslavia's past needs history that is both 'new' (comprehending the whole of human experience) and 'old' ('*wie es eigentlich gewesen ist*'), but it no longer needs a 'Whig interpretation'. The obvious answer would be to live with the past – openly; more secure historical roots would then be found for the future to grow from.

A real understanding of Yugoslavia's history between 1918 and 1988 calls for a completely free enquiry by professional scholars, echoed by a public debate. The regime still thinks it cannot afford it. The politicians and the generals are finding it difficult to accept that there are real advantages to be had in tolerating other opinions, and in listening to arguments. But then, as dogma breeds counter-dogma, and myths anti-myths, historians and the public are also having to learn that lesson. The process, however, has been started. 'Lies are understood by everyone, but truth is very difficult to grasp,' Federico Fellini told a BBC television audience in 1987, in the context of his own artistic interpretation of life. Although truth remains difficult to grasp in the land of the South Slavs, most people there have come to understand, from the late 1970s up to this day, that the lies were only small parts of the truth. Scholars, the public and even the authorities are consciously or subconsciously beginning to live with the past.

The chapters that follow are the outcome of seminars I was invited to conduct in Paris, between 1981 and 1986, at the Ecole des hautes études en sciences sociales, on Yugoslavia and her problems in the context of that country's history since 1918. As Yugoslavia is about to enter the eighth decade of her existence, I imagined it might be useful to take up this material, rewrite it, expand it by additional reading and research here, reduce it to an analytical and comparative framework there, and integrate it around a number of themes that I consider to be germane to her structural history.

Many of the claims to originality once made on Yugoslavia's behalf now appear as spurious. Yet they were easily understood by everyone, even though they were not absolute lies. The outlines of what may be more genuinely the specificity of the Yugoslav 'miracle' are, obviously, more difficult to grasp. Initially, her unification went against the grain of 'Balkanisation', and she had to stand up against the attempts of both Comintern and Axis to re-Balkanise her – until the former changed its line, and the latter was smashed. She then went through a revolution, and pioneered all the modernising and reformist attempts of Communist states. Eventually, she passed on to the Third World not so much her renovated concept of Marxist socialism as the Leninist concept of the one-party state. All this has happened within a well discernible structure of geography, history and culture. Discussing these themes with graduate and research scholars in Paris during my visits there, as well as with my own students of Balkan history at the University of Southampton, has helped me to gain a better understanding of the specificity, the continuity and the distortion of Yugoslav history. I can only hope that students of Central-Eastern European affairs will, in turn, find in these pages some insight into Yugoslavia's problems and her survival.

My acknowledgement is due to *L'Autre Europe*, to the Centre for Security and Conflict Studies, to *Commentaire*, to Scholarly Resources Inc. and to *Vingtième siècle* for permission to use material published by them. My thanks are expressed to the Ecole des hautes études in Paris for inviting me, but, especially, my appreciation goes to the students with whom I work, and who are the only adequate reward left, on both sides of the Channel, for toiling in the universities. This book is for them, and in particular for the one who has typed it scrutinisingly – my son Kosta.

Mount Athos,   ST. K. PAVLOWITCH
September 1987

CONTENTS

CHRONOLOGY OF YUGOSLAVIA'S HISTORY

1918   Unified Kingdom of the Serbs, Croats and Slovenes proclaimed on 1 December.

1919   First general elections held on whole territory of new state with universal manhood suffrage.

1921   Constitution adopted by Constituent Assembly; Communist Party outlawed.

1928   Shots in parliament on 20 June kill or wound a number of Croatian deputies.

1929   King Alexander suspends constitution on 6 January; name of state changed to Kingdom of Yugoslavia.

1931   King grants new constitution.

1934   King Alexander assassinated on 9 October; Peter II succeeds under regency council.

1937   Tito appointed to head Communist Party of Yugoslavia.

1941   Regency and government overthrown on 27 March after acceding to Tripartite Pact; Peter II declared of age; formation of all-party government; Axis Powers attack on 6 April; collapse, occupation and partition of Yugoslavia; resistance and civil war begin.

1943   Jajce Declaration of Anti-Fascist Council for the National Liberation of Yugoslavia on 29 November establishes bases of future Communist regime.

1944   Belgrade liberated by Red Army and Tito's partisans on 20 October.

1945   German troops surrender in Yugoslavia on 15 May; Constituent Assembly, elected from a single list, proclaims Federal People's Republic of Yugoslavia on 29 November.

1946   First Communist constitution adopted.

1948   Communist Party of Yugoslavia expelled from the Cominform on 28 June; break with the Soviet bloc.

1952   Communist Party of Yugoslavia changes its name to League of Communists of Yugoslavia at Sixth Congress.

1953   Second Communist constitution adopted.

1954   Djilas disgraced.

1955   Khrushchev and Bulganin visit Belgrade.

1961   Belgrade Conference of Non-aligned States.

1963   Third Communist constitution adopted; name of state changed to Socialist Federal Republic of Yugoslavia.

1966   Ranković disgraced; Brezhnev visits Yugoslavia.

1968   Student revolt at Belgrade University echoed throughout Yugoslavia; disorders in Kosovo caused by ethnic Albanians.

1974   Fourth, and most elaborate, Communist constitution adopted, brings Yugoslavia near to being a confederation; Tito life president.

1978   Collective leadership implemented at Eleventh Congress.

1980   President Tito dies on 4 May.

1981   Explosion of Albanian nationalism causes extended riots in Kosovo.

1983   First informal re-scheduling of Yugoslavia's foreign debts; 'stabilization' plan adopted.

1987   Record number of strikes disrupts industry; demonstrations by Serbs in Kosovo; Agrokomerc financial scandal.

MAPS

All the three maps overleaf were drawn by Mr A.S. Burn of the Geography Department, University of Southampton.

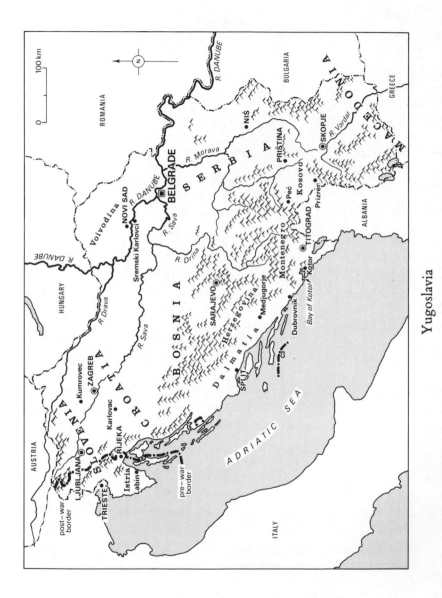

Yugoslavia

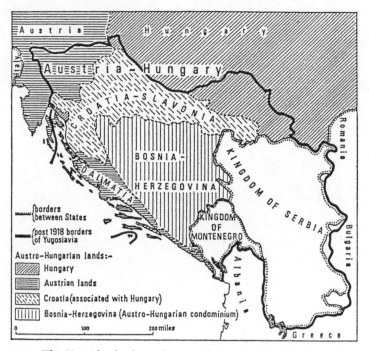

The Yugoslav lands on the eve of the First World War.

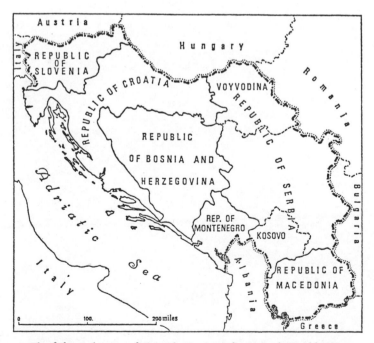

The federated units of Yugoslavia since the Second World War.

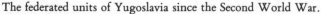

Yes, they lived as neighbours, and they took care lest they should get to know something about each other and become too familiar. Religion, which uplifts the soul under more open skies, has stirred up hatred in these narrow gorges and in these weak heads of ours. Now, unhappy and barren, they groan like wounded animals, they hate each other, and they enjoy it, each one convinced that he is one hundred per cent right, and that the others are one hundred per cent wrong. They feel at ease in their resentment, they fatten on it, and you are sorry to wake them up from their poisoned dream. [. . .]

When they were no longer allowed to indulge in economic competition and in political contest, they came to excel in national controversies, which for little nations, are a way of being spiteful to one's neighbours. Each one considers that the others are to blame for everything, and the one who is most to blame is the one whom you see every day and who shares most of your suffering. Hatred between nations, between little nations, is but an extended version of bad Balkan neighbourliness, where your neighbour is most to blame because you both share the same difficulties. [. . .]

The people will accept everything and, at the same time, do not accept anything. They take what they cannot avoid, and, when they are no longer forced to accept it, all of a sudden, it turns out that, deep in their soul, they had been against it all the time. People are like water; they will get into any vessel, as long as it does not leak, and they can fit into it. When times are bad, they do not look at its form and appearance; the main thing is that they can shelter in it. In doing so, they give some sort of acceptance, under unspecified conditions, and for an unspecified time. Some do it out of fear for the terrible things that occurred in the past, others to keep what they have misappropriated in the dark, others still because they are always on the side of the strong, and all together they contribute to strengthening that Thing, be it as it may, and they are afraid of the unknown that could come in its stead. [. . .]

The Thing is quite indulgent; it does not strictly implement its own laws. If it did, it could send half the citizens to gaol. It is broad-minded, and it does not resort to force, except out of extreme necessity; only now and then does it show what it would be ready to resort to. Things are not too bad, if you think of what it used to be like. One doesn't dare speak openly about what it was like previously; about today, it will be possible to speak tomorrow. In between real freedom, which does not exist anywhere, and real slavery, which does exist and is very real, a middle way has been found, the most human solution – a bearable non-freedom. With endless possibilities of reform and improvement. [. . .]

This summer, he did not sow his garden. He says it is not worth it, that it is cheaper to buy on the market. He has no money, he gets no salary, and he still finds it cheaper to buy than to grow on his own land . . . What he would like best is for someone to pay him a monthly compensation for being alive. Maybe one day, when the world is rich, it could happen – the general pensioning off of individuals, nations, professions and classes. [. . .]

Love, love! You left-wingers talk like teenage girls, I say to Lukić. It isn't a question of love. What we need here is toleration, respect among the nationalities, knowing the others – not love! [. . .]

(translated from Milovan Danolić, *Dragi moj Petroviću*,
Zagreb, 1986)

1

THE HISTORICAL FRAMEWORK – FROM UNIFICATION TO REVOLUTION

The parliamentary monarchy

The development of Yugoslavia evinces one long historical contradiction. Over the centuries, populations tended to blend as a result of their common linguistic origin, of the absence of 'race' in the anthropological sense, and of various influences that had come together in this important geopolitical area. Yet the dominant influences also prevented the blending process from reaching completion. Conquerors moved or harassed populations, drove them away or attracted them, mixed or divided them, but never integrated them. Moreover, the geography that invited intervention from the outside also prevented any native power from expanding, growing, unifying, and checking foreign interference (until the Communist Party turned that geography to good use under Tito in the 1940s).

The conception of Yugoslavia goes back to the 1830s, in the territories of the Habsburg Monarchy where South Slavs – the future Yugoslavs – lived intermingled. It led only slowly to the birth of Yugoslavia, because the power structure impeded it, and because common action was reduced to intellectual dreaming or political scheming. It did not develop along a straight line, and was not predestined to lead to the territorial framework of 1918. Only when Austria-Hungary broke up as a consequence of the First World War did the unification of the Yugoslav lands present itself as a fact of practical politics which did not allow any delay. The approaches to it were divergent. The declarations of politicians had been full of good intentions; for the population at large it corresponded to vague feelings rather than to a clearly expressed national will.

Modern scholarship has yet to consider the question of the peasants' consciousness of their common 'ethnicity' before 1914, or that of the common person's view of the future over the war years to 1918. The Versailles Conference certainly did not invent Yugoslavia. The new state was proclaimed in Belgrade on 1 December 1918 by the crown prince and regent of Serbia, in the presence of members of the Serbian government and of a delegation from the National Council in Zagreb which had become the provisional government for the South Slav territories of the disintegrating Austro-Hungarian Monarchy. Unification was generally accepted, but even the élites were not ready for it when the powers that had kept them divided collapsed.

The Kingdom of the Serbs, Croats and Slovenes – as it was then officially called – was half-way between a nation-state and a fully multi-national community. Its territory was in confusion, much of it devas-tated by warfare, part of it still occupied by foreign troops. Its components were two independent and Serbian-feeling kingdoms that had first united between themselves, and parts of the one-time Dual Monarchy which had also recently declared themselves to be a joint state of the Slovenes, Croats and Serbs. Serbia and Montenegro both included territories that had been Turkish up till the Balkan Wars of 1912–13, while the former Habsburg dominions had been governed by four dif-ferent constitutional structures – including Croatia with its home rule.

The continued territorial crisis postponed the calling of a constituent assembly until November 1919. Yet a central combined government was established which tackled, right from the start, the task of making the land of the Serbs, Croats and Slovenes theirs both to live in and own. The self-determination of peoples and the peasant ownership of the soil were Balkan ideals that were radical for the dominions of the historic empires that were collapsing, and they were the new principles on which Yugo-slavia was established. When its borders were eventually settled, they contained some 12 million inhabitants – of whom, however, two million were non-Slavs – leaving out at least half a million South Slavs, mostly in Italy. Over a quarter of all the arable land would be redis-tributed to over a quarter of the total number of peasant families.

However revolutionary in terms of national unification and of land-ownership, the élites on all sides were conservative in their political conceptions. They went on as if 1918 had simply been the outcome of the limited aims they had been trying realistically to achieve in 1914. For the Serbian state, this had been the liberation of the remaining unredeemed lands; for the Croatian political class, the ultimate improvement on Croatia's autonomous status. Yugoslavia, however, was neither an extension of the kingdom of Serbia nor a South Slav version of Austria-Hungary.

In the elections to the Constituent Assembly, Democrats and Radicals emerged as the largest groups, with just under 20 and 17 per cent of the electorate respectively. The new Democratic Party, representing votes from all regions, rejected sectional interests as a basis for political action.

It advocated a centralist parliamentary government and land reform to level out political and social differences. The old Serbian Radical Party, which had been in power in Serbia since 1903, not only retained its hold over the peasantry of the old kingdom, but attracted a large proportion of the Serbs of the former Habsburg provinces. The Croatian Peasant Party (HSS, *Hrvatska seljačka stranka*) gained over 14 per cent – the votes of the newly-enfranchished Croatian peasantry. The infant Communist Party focussed discontent, made full use of economic difficulties, and polled over 12 per cent of disparate protest votes.

The Radical-Democratic coalition decided that the constitutional document would be passed by a simple majority, which led to a HSS boycott, and this weakened the Croatian cause from the start. Eventually endorsed by a majority of 27 on the full strength of the assembly, the Constitution of 28 June 1921 merely updated the old Serbian structure of a parliamentary government under a monarchy, retaining the triple name of the state as a concession to non-Serbian feeling. It marked the triumph of the centralist Serbian experience over the Austro-Hungarian tradition of constitutional complexity.

To the Moscow-operated Communist International (Comintern) the South Slav kingdom appeared as just another territorial enlargement in the wake of the imperialist Great War, that of a victorious Serbia at the expense of a defeated Austria-Hungary. It considered the satisfied Serbs to be non-revolutionary material, and looked for allies among the other nationalities of Yugoslavia, but it overestimated the revolutionary potential of the situation. As the Communists' opposition turned to terrorism, the public mood towards them changed. The government was able to outlaw their party in 1921, while the HSS boycott rallied more and more Croats against the Constitution. It was thus under not altogether favourable auguries that the parliamentary system began to function. The multiplicity and diversity of parties anyhow spelt government by unstable coalitions, and created an important role for royal arbitration, especially as this was undertaken by a man of the standing of Alexander, regent, then formally sovereign on the death of his father King Peter I in 1921.

Though voted by a clear majority, the Constitution was unacceptable to, or not to the liking of, many others. Between intransigence and boycott more and more Democrats began to see the need for a third way, and eventually they parted with the Radicals. The elections of 1923, held on the issue of a revision of the Constitution, merely hardened differences. Radicals and HSS came out on top, while the Democrats, who were more dispersed regionally, lost out in the middle. In 1924 the ageing Radical prime minister Pašić had to give way to the Democrat-based cabinet under Davidović, who extended a hand to the HSS, and thus brought the latter's boycott to an end. Accepted with reluctance by King Alexander and by the HSS leader Radić, Davidović barely survived a hundred days in office. Pašić returned and bargained for the continued existence of an administration based on shifting coalitions, which split the Democrats, and produced extraordinary switches of loyalty, but furthered neither the consciousness of national unity nor the higher interests of the state.

After Pašić's final resignation and death in 1926, his tactics were continued by his Radical successors, until by 1928 the parliamentary system seemed to be falling down. In June of that year, insults were answered with revolver shots in parliament. Radić was mortally wounded. Opinion was numbed. The HSS called for an extra-parliamentary cabinet to be appointed by the king, to start a process leading to a new and practically dualist constitution. On 6 January 1929, King Alexander dissolved parliament, suspended the Constitution by autocratic proclamation, and appointed a new government.

The first confused decade of Yugoslavia's history was over. Its political system had not been able to establish a compromise between the interests of nationalities and regions within a national (or 'supra-national') Yugoslav party system before the authoritarian monarch declared his impatience with it. And yet the parliamentary governments had governed. They had also produced more gratifying and lasting results in the economic and diplomatic fields. Foreign policy had aimed at securing the frontiers that had been obtained. With Czechoslovakia and Romania, Yugoslavia had concluded in 1920-1 the Little Entente treaties to prevent Hungary from trying to destroy the peace settlement, and the Habsburgs from attempting a restoration. The two endeavours were considered as closely linked by the three partners, all successor-states of Austria-Hungary. Even though the advent of Fascism meant that Italy remained a major danger, Mussolini was not yet ready to push things too far, and a new *modus vivendi* was reached in 1924 between the two Adriatic states. France was the one power that stood firm on the territorial clauses of the peace treaties. She had linked herself to the Little Entente in order to offset Italy's friendship with Hungary and her increasing stake in Albania. In general Yugoslavia, along with her partners, tried to make for herself a place in the new European order acting with and through the League of Nations and its agencies.

Economic policy had aimed at reinforcing the country's integration and its independence. Yugoslavia quickly put her economic house in order after the initial postwar chaos. Her leaders did recognise the backward nature of their societies, and had visions of a radical transformation in the future. They managed to solve the social side of the land question through an agrarian reform that brought the rural structure throughout the kingdom to follow the model of peasant ownership in pre-war Serbia, which was also the ideal of the new peasant parties. Even though agriculture made a rapid recovery, the extreme fragmentation of rural property made it difficult to increase productivity. Miserable poverty co-existed with relatively favourable peasant incomes. The economic problem was that the land had to provide a living for too many people.

As net emigration absorbed no more than 13 per cent of the total increase in population during that first decade, the government sought to stimulate industry in the face of faith in a mythical peasant way of life which continued steadfastly. It invested in the state-owned sectors and, since domestic capital was limited, it attracted foreign capital from friendly countries. War reparations were useful as they were mostly paid in capital goods, and received in the years of greatest need. A cautious financial policy enabled Yugoslavia to repay her war debts by the end of 1926. The subsequent stabilisation of the dinar opened the way to an influx of capital. The trade balance was favourable during 1924–6, while the development of shipping and tourism provided an appreciable aid to the balance of payments. Improving economic conditions and social legislation also helps to explain why workers were less inclined to rally round any Communist-controlled movement after 1921.

The authoritarian monarchy

The royal coup provoked no real protest at first. It had been announced as a temporary expedient to mark time until passions had subsided, and people were not sorry to have a respite from politics. The new government was initially helped by economic conditions. Successful efforts were made to encourage the spread of smallholder co-operatives, to educate farmers in the use of more modern techniques, to diversify and specialise, to develop and rationalise exports. Such conditions were short-lived, however, for in 1931 the economy generally began to deteriorate.

The regime claimed that it had saved the state. It had officially adopted the name Yugoslavia, and accelerated the integration of administration and legislation. Its efforts to merge Serbian, Croatian and Slovenian feelings into one Yugoslav patriotism offered the possibility of influencing coming generations, but separate traditions could not be eradicated overnight. Different sections of public opinion had expected different things from a temporary suspension of constitutional government, and were subsequently disappointed. To the Croats, it appeared as a more efficient way of getting them to accept Serbian-style centralism, and it increased the emotional separation from government in Belgrade that Radić's death had caused. The secessionist Ustasha (*Ustaša*) movement would grow out of the radical fringe of Croatian dissatisfaction. It was increasingly inspired by Nazism and Fascism, and operated from abroad. As for the people of Serbia, for the sake of what to many other Yugoslavs appeared as Serbian hegemony, they had been made to give up the political liberties they had become accustomed to over the past quarter of a century.

In September 1931, the King granted a new constitution which legalised most of his special powers. The full effect of the world economic crisis hit Yugoslavia at the time when disappointment was turning to unrest. Agricultural prices fell to their lowest level in 1933–4, and the dinar was depreciated by one-third of its value by 1935. Part of the trouble was that the country's trade pattern did not coincide with its diplomatic alignment, as most of its exchanges were with Italy, Austria and Germany. Yet, far from thinking of changing alliances, King Alexander not only turned the Little Entente into a formal pact in 1933, but linked it to other Balkan states the following year, when a Balkan Entente was concluded as another regional organisation between Greece, Romania, Turkey and Yugoslavia. He also aimed at setting up a diplomatic network gravitating towards France, in order to balance the one being constructed by Italy around Yugoslavia's borders, but whereas the king's foreign policy had been quite successful, the same could not be said of the domestic results of his personal rule – except that, in the eyes of Yugoslavia's supporters and enemies alike, he had come to be identified with his state.

On 9 October 1934, at the start of a state visit to France, he was assassinated by an Ustasha agent. The murder caused dismay, but provoked no disruption. The Constitution of 1931, tailored for King Alexander personally, survived to function even without a monarch, under a regency headed by Prince Paul (Alexander's cousin) for the child King Peter II. The worst had not happened after Alexander's death, and the regency basically continued the personal regime. With a new royal person at the helm who did not have the late king's prestige and character, it went on to manoeuvre with and between the party leaderships.

With the disruption of traditional trade patterns during the depression, Yugoslavia came to depend more and more on Germany as her main customer and supplier, with short-term economic benefits. Agricultural prices rose again, and so did production. The currency recovered, and the government was able to stimulate considerable industrial development. However, the opposition was raising its head again. The country was tired of veiled authoritarianism and pseudo-representation. As the Soviet Union no longer thought that the break-up of Yugoslavia would serve its interests, and as Communism became a respectable 'progressive' force against Fascism, Tito was appointed to take over the Communist Party of Yugoslavia, and turned to restoring order in its organisation after December 1937. Living partly in the dream-world of the Communist society of the future, and partly in expectation of an immediate world revolution which would integrate the Yugoslav lands in a universal union of Communist republics, the party leaderships would apply Stalin's successive tactical moves, while the main political development in Yugoslavia went not in that direction, but in the tightening up of the United Opposition coalition under Maček – Radić's successor at the head of the HSS.

Calling for a national government to work out transitional arrangements leading to a new constitution, which would satisfy a majority of Serbs, a majority of Croats and a majority of Slovenes, it caused a wave of enthusiasm. Serbo-Croatian relations at popular level had never been so close, as the opposition coalition made headway in the general elections of the late thirties (more than 37 per cent of the votes in 1935; almost 45 per cent in 1938) in spite of a system designed to favour the government.

Both government and opposition agreed on the need to solve the Croatian problem before a European crisis placed Yugoslavia, and all her components, in danger. Eventually, in August 1939, the HSS alone came to an agreement with the regency, thus breaking off its alliance with the Serbian opposition parties. The existing legislature was dissolved, and a self-governing Province of Croatia was set up on the basis of the Crown's reserved emergency powers. Croatia, with its special status, would be the preserve of the popular and moderate HSS for the next twenty months or so. While Maček felt it urgent to counter the Ustasha appeal of secession, the Serbian opposition leaders saw the agreement as a half-measure which separated Croats from Serbs at a time when unity was essential.

The Croatian compromise had been reached under the pressure of European events. Feeling that regional alliances could not protect Yugoslavia against Italy without adequate support from Britain and France, whose attitude was at best ambivalent, the regency government had veered to a policy of neutrality in 1936. Prince Paul's tactics then turned him temporarily to the Axis while his strategy looked ultimately to the West, but the tactics increasingly hamstrung the strategy. The growing strength of Germany and Italy, added to the benefits of the German economic connexion, made real neutrality difficult.

The beginning of the Second World War increased Yugoslavia's dependence on the Reich, even before the fall of France made it plain to all how perilously isolated and weak her position had become. As German pressure grew, on 25 March 1941 Yugoslavia joined the 'satellites': she adhered to the Tripartite Pact by which Germany, Italy and Japan had agreed to share out the leadership of a new order in Europe and Greater East Asia. Two days later, on 27 March, a bloodless military coup brought the regency to an end. Although the cabinet had been joined by representatives of various parties, it did not command the loyalty of a substantial portion of the nation, which felt increasingly demoralised. Serbian public opinion, in particular, had totally lost confidence in Prince Paul, his ministers and their policies. By late March 1941, tension had reached a point where the coup probably forestalled a revolt, disorders, or a disintegration of the army.

In fact, the coup brought together all party leaders in a broad coalition government, formed in a constitutional near-vacuum and in the middle of a foreign policy crisis. It showed a deep yearning for a fully representative government in an hour of need, but could only paper over the differences between the various political conceptions it encompassed within the new executive. The coalition cabinet was not given the time to work out a policy towards the Axis, let alone towards the constitutional problem. As far as Hitler was concerned, Yugoslavia had proved unreliable and hostile, and she had to be liquidated. Attacked without a declaration of war on 6 April, the country was stunned and quickly put out of action. By the time of the capitulation of its armed forces on 18 April, King Peter and his government had already gone into exile, soon to join the other Allied leaders in London, with their country's unresolved problems in their bags.

It had taken a world war for it to come prematurely into the world at the end of 1918 and, however shaky its state of health in the spring of 1941, it took another world war to destroy the Kingdom of Yugoslavia which, to all intents and purposes, came to an end between 6 and 18 April of that year. The common enterprise of the South Slavs would have been a difficult one even if attempted in the best possible conditions. As it was, the abnormal strains created by population growth and the multiplicity of traditions, the world economic crisis and the appearance of totalitarian ideologies, imposed impossible burdens on the somewhat clumsy grouping together in imitation of West European forms. Both Fascism and Communism offered alternative patterns for the reorganisation of government and society. The political class did not, however, turn to these, and what the royalist dictatorship of the 1930s was out to achieve – in Yugoslavia as elsewhere in the Balkans – was to protect the *status quo* by going back to older methods at a time of international tension. When Europe was once again plunged into war, Prince-Regent Paul manoeuvred frantically but in vain to keep the fighting away from the realm he kept in trust. When the crunch came, he found himself without the support of a broad political platform.

Serbs and Croats, the two largest historically-conscious groups, were nearest to each other culturally and territorially, but the former had reacted as a satisfied majority within the framework of the combined state, which had not turned out as the latter had envisaged. Failing to find any other solution that would satisfy the Croats without changing the structure of the state, the Crown had brought the parliamentary regime to an end, and tried to foster a feeling of Yugoslav patriotism from above. Thus, in the difficult decade of the 1930s, the Serbo-Croatian problem was removed from public political dialogue. It was discussed through contacts between opposition parties which wanted to combine in order to challenge the authoritarian regime, or between the Crown and part of the opposition so as to divide the opposition.

The Constitution granted by King Alexander had survived him intact for almost five years before it was all but destroyed between August 1939 and April 1941, when the compromise with the HSS introduced an element of dualism and, in fact, initiated a process of revision, before Peter II was made to assume the royal prerogative six months ahead of his formal coming of age. The coup of 27 March 1941 could not have done anything to ward off, or prepare for, Hitler's intervention, which would have occurred anyway, sooner or later, to sort out the Yugoslav situation. Nor did the coup contribute to the final outcome of the Second

World War – as Yugoslavs like to think – by disrupting Hitler's plans against the Soviet Union.

War and civil war

The Yugoslav state was said by the enemy to have been annihilated along with its armed forces. The Germans wanted to control the main communication lines and mineral deposits, and to crush the Serbs – whom Hitler considered to be disturbers of the European order. All claims at the expense of regions inhabited by them were accepted, all separatisms encouraged, all tensions exasperated. The Ustashas were allowed to set up a nominally independent state of Croatia (NDH, *Nezavisna Država Hrvatska*) over the various territories inhabited by Croats (thus taking in Bosnia and Herzegovina), except that Italy took a large part of the coast, and the NDH contained almost as many 'aliens' as Catholic Croats. Furthermore, what had been Yugoslavia was divided into a German zone and an Italian zone.

In the spring of 1941, the British had felt for a while that the conquering might of the Axis could be tackled. The Belgrade coup had contributed to this, and the several risings in occupied Yugoslavia that summer were seen as a sequel. But the exiled government was soon paralysed by old issues hideously magnified by events, and the risings were not what they had at first seemed to be in Allied London. The political leaders who had sought refuge in Britain failed to provide leadership, even when they were looked up to from Yugoslavia, where people had risen either in self-defence or because they had believed that powerful help was forthcoming.

The Ustashas' ferocious racialism in the NDH caused the Serbian peasantry to defend their lives. Montenegro stood up against the Italian attempt to set up a separate client-state. In Serbia, an upsurge of pro-Allied enthusiasm at the time of Hitler's invasion of Russia produced an insurrection against the Germans, who retaliated ruthlessly. It was there that two groups emerged with designs that were more than merely local. Colonel Mihailović's, with debris of the regular army, aimed at reorganising a clandestine movement loyal to the exiled government that would promote him to the rank of general. Tito's, with the Communist Party cadres, was grabbing with both hands the opportunity given by the destruction of the Yugoslav state to advance the cause of the revolution. The strife that quickly developed between the two enabled the Germans to restore apparent order with less effort than expected.

As military repression exploded the bubble of insurgent optimism in eastern Yugoslavia, the popular mood turned against the Communists. Tito and his partisans were saved by their 'long march' to the other end of the country, where the poor peasantry of Bosnia had been most affected by the traumas of defeat and massacre. Thereafter, the revolutionary conflict waged by the Communist Party gained its own momentum in the civil strife that ravaged Yugoslavia for the rest of the war. Mihailović kept his base in Serbia, a region of ethnic, religious, and even social homogeneity (with its relatively prosperous smallholders dominant), but he went underground. Realising with his staff officer's background that no second European front would be started for at least another year, he would concentrate on preparing the groundwork for a rising to be launched when the Allies were near enough to make it worthwhile. He would also try and bring together all those forces outside Serbia that could contribute to strengthening his movement. He envisaged it as a military service, loyal to the old Yugoslav state, and wanted to avoid useless sacrifices.

Left to their own devices in 1942, as Allied interest in the Yugoslav resistance lessened, the insurgents survived by mimicry and mobility, extending their constituencies and fighting each other. They first called themselves chetniks, after the *četnik* irregulars of earlier wars against the Turks, but if they were taken over or organised by the Communists they were partisans. Divided increasingly into 'partisans' and 'nationalists', they adhered to, or made use of the names of, one or other of the more ambitious movements whom Mihailović and Tito preferred to call respectively the Yugoslav Home Army (JVO, *Jugoslovenska vojska u otadžbini*) and the People's Liberation Movement (NOP, *Narodnooslobo-dilački pokret*). Both were at first expressions of an essentially Serbian resistance, for it was Serbs alone whom the Axis treated collectively as a vanquished foe.

Possibilities of action were greater in the Italian than in the German zone. Although they were Italy's allies, the Nazis and Ustashas were in fact her rivals on the other side of the Adriatic. The problems of Italian implantation in the coastal province of Dalmatia were dependent on the increased chaos in Ustasha-controlled (or uncontrolled) territory, where Italian troops had to intervene to halt the massacres of Orthodox Serbs, to prevent the latter from exacting retribution on Catholic Croats (and on Muslims in between), and to stop the insurgency from spreading to the coast. In order to end the bloodbath in the NDH, Italian commanders had extended their military presence to most of their zone. They had done it by coming to terms with many of the Serbian rebels, who welcomed their protection against the Ustashas, and who were ready to resist the increasing spread of the Communist partisans.

These chetniks of the Italian zone were nevertheless anxious, in 1942, to acknowledge Mihailović as a nominal supreme authority so as to legitimise their position in the eyes of the population. He took the risk, for although he could not, as a Yugoslav officer, condone their increasingly open collaboration, as a Serb and as an individual he felt a good deal of understanding for their position. He knew (as indeed did the Italians) that they would never oppose the British, while they kept the Communists in check, and made the JVO appeal more widespread. He believed that the Western Allies would land, and in the mean time he hoped that he could influence the local chetnik captains to mend their ways. The gamble was lost, for he had no effective authority over them, and they were increasingly dependent on the Italians. His undertaking made it difficult for him to find an audience among Croats, there was no landing in Yugoslavia, and Communist propaganda turned it all against him. Out of the complex patterns of 1942, Tito's movement, which had been almost destroyed in the east, emerged like a phoenix in the west.

At the end of that year, outside interest in Yugoslavia increased. When the Allied victories over the Axis powers in North Africa opened the way for an assault on 'Fortress Europe', more importance began to be attached to diversionary action in the Balkans. The Axis had to be led astray on the location of an Allied landing. With the impending threat of a Balkan front, the Germans feared that the latent insurgency in the NDH could turn into a danger for the whole peninsula, while Mihailović could link together numerous loose formations biding their time to strike against the Axis. They wanted to eliminate all insurgents quickly but they could only do it with the Italians, who had different ideas on how to control the area, and who were increasingly disenchanted with the war. Italian generals did not believe in the success of large-scale anti-guerilla operations (the brunt of which they had borne hitherto), and they were anxious to keep contacts which could perhaps have been extended to the Anglo-Americans when they had landed.

The German-directed encirclement operations of January-March 1943 were a military defeat for Tito, and they considerably weakened Mihailović, but the failure of the Axis to weld a united front made it impossible to achieve a lasting solution. During that time, both the Communist leader and the king's general also fought desperately for control of the Adriatic hinterland, each one anxious to destroy the other before the presumed British landing, which the former dreaded and the latter hoped for. The entanglement of antagonisms and arrangements between the different sides became increasingly complicated and bloody.

By the time of the Allied invasion of Italy in June 1943, the British were demanding more of Mihailović than he was able or willing to give without adequate support, and they were turning to Tito as an additional or alternative source of support – in order to exploit every opportunity of involving the enemy on the other side of the Adriatic. The collapse of Italy in September brought about the deflation of the local chetnik formations that were dependent on the Italian army, and the partisans were strengthened by the capture of Italian military stock. Mihailović, who had engaged in only limited action against the Germans since the end of 1941, emerged again in the latter half of 1943 to the point where he has been estimated to have led the second most active resistance movement in Europe after Tito's. While the Germans continued to believe that he would turn out to be the leader of a nationwide insurgency as soon as the Allies came anywhere near Yugoslavia, the British and Americans came to be convinced of the effective superiority of Tito and, in order to get more out of him, came to accept his view – that the NOP was not just the more effective resistance, but the only one. By the time they had definitely turned to Tito in November, the Allied advance had slowed down in Italy, and the Germans had recovered their balance in Yugoslavia. All resistance was again drastically reduced over the winter of 1943–4.

The NOP had fattened on the NDH, where it had harnessed the plight of the western Serbs, then infiltrated the disappointed army and administration of the Ustasha regime, and eventually offered a way out to the increasing number of Croats who wanted to leave that sinking boat. But it still did not cut much ice in the east generally. While the Germans carried out an ordered evacuation from the Balkans through Serbia in the summer of 1944, there was fighting between the partisans trying to force their way into Mihailović's home territory, and the chetniks trying to fend them off, but there was no large-scale resistance. Then, in September, as the Red Army reached Yugoslavia's eastern borders, there was a sudden rise in the military operations of the resistance against the Germans. Soviet forces helped the partisans to free Belgrade and install themselves in the capital earlier than they could have done otherwise, and went on to Hungary, leaving the Yugoslavs to liberate the rest of their country by themselves, and fight their civil war to an end. The war against Germany continued for another seven months after the fall of Belgrade. It did not end until 15 May 1945, a full week after Germany's official surrender.

The resistance in Yugoslavia was a patriotic insurgency which made life tougher for the invaders, but could do them no lasting damage. The various chetnik, or nationalist, groups represented the last traditional Balkan guerilla, local and seasonal. At a higher level, they were also an officers' movement trying to mould them into an organised fighting force. Over and above them all stood Mihailović, a father-figure who provided the symbolic authority that held together their loose company, but who followed events more than he could initiate them. His support was drawn from those who viewed change as a threat. His strategy was geared to liberation by regular Allied forces.

The occupation system, however, attempted to impose a brutal peace, mainly on the country's Serbian population, but without the strength to enforce it – an ideal situation for the propagation of a revolutionary movement. The partisans fought a revolutionary war in a constantly shifting pattern, and their leadership did so with clear political aims. Tito placed a patriotic movement in the service of world Communism, with the object of destroying all forces that opposed the transformation of the war of liberation into a war for the establishment of Communist rule. The Communist Party obtained the support of a significant part of the population – those who had been radicalised by the upheavals of war. The old élites, who had political experience, who had had power, and who had been more than a match for Communist tactics until the war, were first divided and demoralised, then weakened and disorientated, and eventually destroyed, both by the Nazis and their wartime ideological allies, and in the course of the civil war. As the Germans withdrew, there was a power vacuum which the Communists rapidly filled.

During the Second World War, the conquerors of Yugoslavia not only destroyed the state, but they set its components against each other in an unprecedented way, for never before had there been physical conflict among the Yugoslav peoples as such. An infernal cycle of large-scale massacres was started soon after the partition when, installed as rulers of an inflated and nominally independent Croatian satellite, the Ustashas had attempted a 'final solution' to the question of the Eastern Orthodox Serbs in their midst. The latter had risen in self-defence – as chetniks or partisans who had gone on to do their best, there and elsewhere, to eliminate each other and their supporters, while facing up to periodic anti-insurgent operations organised by the Germans with a brutality that stemmed from their general attitude to the Slavs, who shared with the Jews the base of the pyramid of Nazi racial theory. Yugoslavs were, nevertheless, slaughtered by other Yugoslavs more than by foreign soldiers. Yet the outcome of the war led again to a united Yugoslavia, even though once again there was no national consultation. The defeat of the Axis had destroyed the chances of those native movements that had thought of a solution by withdrawing into the confines of sectional nationalism under foreign protection.

Without the coup of 27 March 1941, without the resistance – however confused and fratricidal – Yugoslavia might have disappeared from the map of Europe, and she would probably not have been able to maintain her independence in the post-war world.

o

2

THE HISTORICAL FRAMEWORK – FROM
STALINISM TO THE DEMISSION OF TITOISM

Stalinist and Titoist Communism

In order to strengthen the international position of the new regime they
had already put into operation, the Communist leaders made some trans-
itory cosmetic concessions, including the acceptance of a regency and of a
provisional government under Marshal (since 1943) Tito in March 1945.
Although victorious in the civil war, they were still uncertain of themselves – they feared the West, particularly the British, they feared the
class enemy, however broken up, and, more than anything else, they
feared a combination of the two. The victorious People's Liberation
Army ended the cycle of massacres started four years earlier by doing
away, in the last days of the war, with more of their opponents who had
followed the retreating Germans into Austria, only to be sent back into
Yugoslavia by the British. This last wave of victims was made up of the
native units, armed by the occupation authorities to fight the Communists, and of their 'camp followers'. Bands of guerillas were still at large,
but there was no possible confrontation between the disorganised and
mutually incompatible anti-Communist groups and the Communist
Party in whose hands the reins of power were already firmly held.

A Constituent Assembly was elected with the right quasi-unanimity
of votes. On 23 November 1945 – the second anniversary of the NOP
Anti-Fascist Council that had opposed the king's return and made Tito a
Marshal – the Federal People's Republic of Yugoslavia was proclaimed
by acclamation, and a constitution, modelled on Stalin's of 1936, was
unanimously adopted on 31 January 1946. It was Yugoslavia's third, and
the first in a series of Communist fundamental laws. It sanctioned the
country's new structure as a multinational federation of eight units, on
both ethnic and historical criteria, which was intended to establish a
balance between them, to avoid the division of territory with inter-
twined communities, and to provide a special status for the two regions
associated with Serbia that contained a mix of Yugoslavs and of a substantial overspill from neighbouring nationalities.

In fact all power emanated from the Communist Party under a

quadrumvirate made up of Tito – whose cult was consciously organised – with Djilas, Kardelj and Ranković. In that revolutionary period, Yugoslavia lived under a repressive dogmatic regime. As armed resistance gradually shrank to armed bands, widely-publicised trials eliminated a whole range of opponents, real or potential, from General Mihailović (executed in July 1946) and Archbishop Stepinac (sentenced to prison in October) downwards.

Once again, the country had emerged devastated from the conflict, yet reconstruction was carried out on an essentially political basis. The destruction of the propertied classes was one of the aims of the new regime's economic policy. The bourgeoisie presented no great problem: it had already largely been destroyed by the war. The peasantry was more difficult to tackle: the partisans were peasants, and the smallholders' produce was badly needed. Although collectivisation of the land was not immediately imposed, Yugoslavia moved faster in that direction than the other Communist-led states of Eastern Europe. In 1947, also well ahead of the others, she introduced long-range planning in order to become an independent industrial power. Production was not yet back to pre-war levels, the capital equipment and industrial material needed were far beyond the country's capacity to produce, nor could they be paid for by exports from the distrustful agricultural sector, but revolutionary ardour would make up for all that the war-battered economy lacked.

Foreign policy was no less dynamic. It attempted to force the decisions of the peace conference, to round off the South Slavs' ethnic domain at the expense of Italy and Austria, but since the Western Allies no longer looked favourably on Communist Yugoslavia, she obtained no more than the Istrian peninsula in February 1947 (when the peace treaty with Italy was eventually signed). Trieste and its territory became pawns in the Cold War. Towards the south-east, her policy was well and truly expansionist. The very concept of federation left it open to new members, and by the end of that year the dream of a Yugoslav-led Balkan federation seemed to be moving towards reality.

The Yugoslav leaders were proud of their achievements during and since the war. They were active in promoting the aims of Communism in their own country, and enthusiastic about the new Communist Information Bureau (Cominform) set up in 1947. The difference between Yugoslavia and other East European states in these post-war years lay in the extent of Tito's hold over his regime, and in his country's position bordering on the Mediterranean and on non-Communist Europe. This combination would be the cause of difficulties both with neighbours and

with the Soviet Union. Because of increasing tension in Europe, Stalin
wanted to prevent the development of a situation likely to cause trouble
in the Communist camp that he was setting up. His need to be able to
control Yugoslavia more directly because of her geopolitical position led
to the break.

The men who ruled Yugoslavia had not seen it coming, and had
certainly not wanted it. In spite of the shock produced by their party's
expulsion from the Cominform in 1948 and by the clash with the Soviet
Union, they instinctively clung to power with a mixture of naïvety and
shrewdness. On the whole, the leadership picked by Tito in the late
1930s stuck together, and the instruments of power remained in the
hands of that group. The Soviet threat strengthened its position in the
population at large as it was able to capitalise both on a patriotism derived
from fear of the Russians and on the patriotism of the revolutionary war.
A Fifth Party Congress was held – the first since the revolution – to
show that the Communist Party of Yugoslavia was united behind its
leaders, to legitimise it independently of the Soviet Union, and to
reinforce Tito's position. One of the consequences of the removal of
Stalin as the transcendental inspirer was to increase the cult of the Yugoslav leader's personality. No chances were taken. As the number of
political trials increased, the security services turned their attention to
Communist as well as non-Communist subversion, and police terror
ensured an all-risks guarantee of loyalty within the Party and at large. By
1950 Stalin had tried all methods save military intervention to overthrow
Tito, but this last step had become too dangerous, for the West had
decided, as a calculated risk, to come to the help of Yugoslavia.

The country's economic ambitions, and her economy, were collapsing. Western help in the 1950s (estimated at over $2,000 million in the
form of outright grants) enabled Yugoslavia to withstand economic and
military pressure from the Soviet Union and its allies. It also helped her
to put up with the consequences of her own imitation-Stalinist plan, and
to make concessions to economic realities. There was a shift of emphasis
from intimidation to persuasion. Self-management institutions were
evolved which aimed at giving people (at least those integrated in the
system) the feeling that they participated in the local day-to-day decision-
making process.

To endorse the changes, and to make them appear as an advance
towards socialism rather than as a tactical retreat, a Sixth Congress was
held in 1952. The event was both an anti-Stalinist demonstration and a
solemnisation of a further development of Marxism symbolised by a

change of name – from Communist Party to League of Communists of Yugoslavia. In January 1953 a new Constitutional Law correspondingly adopted the machinery of 1946 to the needs of the regime's experimental phase. The office of President of the Republic was instituted for Tito, and a beginning was made to theorising about a 'socialist direct democracy' that rejected both Stalinist state socialism and bourgeois pluralist democracy. All this had deep political consequences. While outside the Party many felt more relaxed, within it people sank into passivity or, following the lead of Djilas at the very top, wanted to move on to more open forms of socialism.

In foreign relations too, a reluctant Tito was beginning to commit himself to the West in return for protection until, with Stalin's death in 1953, there appeared again the possibility of influencing developments in the Communist world. Djilas's disgrace in 1954, and his three trials in 1955–7, followed by ten years' imprisonment, symbolised the end of liberalisation. Although there was no return to the methods of government of the late 1940s, an uneasy period of stricter controls followed, in the economic field no less than the political. By expanding his contacts with the post-colonial world, Tito hoped to satisfy his longing for a world role, and to envisage a relationship with Stalin's heirs that would not affect his independence. In the initial period of indecision following the break with Stalin, he had sought to find his bearings while maintaining an equidistant position between East and West. This had made him sensitive to the changing balance of world forces. The Yugoslavs had turned to developing contacts they had made when they were playing an important role in the Cominform, and had then broadened these out. By associating with the 'Third World', Tito could hope to play down his increasing dependence on the 'First World', look forward to a reconciliation with the new leaders of the 'Second World', and satisfy his foreign policy ambitions.

Relations with the Soviet bloc improved, leading to the visit to Belgrade of Khrushchev and Bulganin in 1955, and to Tito's return visit to Moscow the following year, after a reconciliation on equal terms was achieved. In the de-Stalinising process, there was much misunderstanding, with the Soviet leadership and with the satellites, fraught as they were with the Polish and Hungarian crises of 1956. Tito, no less than Khrushchev, was anxious that the process be ordered and channelled. He was concerned that relations with the West should continue, so that Yugoslavia should not be trapped into renewed subordination to Moscow. He strengthened the connection with the Third World, where

Yugoslav influence was to culminate in the 1961 Belgrade conference of non-aligned states.

While it trod the broad way of multifarious socialism abroad, the Titoist regime kept to the narrower path of monopolistic Communism at home, as was seen in the long-delayed Seventh Congress of 1958. This also emphasised the government's careful attempt to create a climate in which some measure of 'Yugoslavism' could again be made to grow. The feelings of sectional difference had not gone away. One could even say that they had been sharpened by the impossibility of fostering anything common to all Yugoslavs other than Communism. In the 1950s, they had re-emerged with decentralisation, infiltrated the federal structure, and become a readily available mode for the emotional expression of dissatisfaction with issues of all sorts. The republics, however, were not co-terminous with nations, and there were anyway 'favoured' and 'disfavoured' nationalisms. Serbian nationalism was linked with hegemony over the community, and Croatian nationalism with separatism from the community. All this led the government, in the mid-1950s, to try to restore some Yugoslav consciousness, albeit a socialist one, above national feelings.

At the end of 1956, ten years had passed since the first five-year plan. Its aims had been attained for the most part, however high the price. A second five-year plan, more realistic and more flexible, was started in 1957, and completed one year ahead of schedule, at the end of 1960. The years between 1947 and 1961 had seen significant progress, at the same time as they had made the internal difficulties of the system glaringly evident. Through the nationalisation of the means of production and forced extensive industrialisation, a solution of sorts had been found to the twin problems of rural overpopulation and of dependence on foreign capital. The pre-war level of wages had been surpassed after 1960. Communism had succeeded in achieving an industrial take-off, but it had done so with the help of massive economic aid from the capitalist West – thus bringing in again through the back door dependence on foreign capital. Centralised planning had outlived any purpose it had ever had. Workers' self-management of enterprises had been a brilliant idea – which might have provided a motive force to set the economy moving again from the sandbank on to which it had been wedged by the speed of its acceleration, had it not remained purely formal for fifteen years after its inception. The Yugoslav government was bringing itself to face new and more real economic reforms.

The contradictions of Titoism

The lack of immediate and spectacular success in Tito's policy towards the Soviet Union, the restoration of relative order at home, the need for ever more Western aid, had all driven the Yugoslav leadership back to a position where it needed to make its rule more acceptable. The 1960s were characterised by a continuous tug of war between reformists and conservatives. The former were economic realists who wanted efficiency; the latter were political realists out to protect the power basis. That climate was marked by the freeing of Djilas at the beginning of 1961, his return to prison the following year, and his final discharge in 1966. The reforms of the 1950s had been half-measures, incompletely carried through, with brakes applied at the first sign of difficulties. Those of 1961 were intended gradually to supplant direct price-fixing with fiscal and monetary policies, as a controlled experiment which would not detract from the regime's long-term aims. A divided and hesitant team saw the need for more productive competence, yet feared the political consequences of economic efficiency.

In order to harmonise the complex developments of the previous ten years, a new constitutional statute was promulgated in April 1963 for the promoted Socialist (from 'People's', which had in turn replaced 'Democratic') Federal Republic of Yugoslavia. It was based on a theory of double sovereignty of working people and nations. Personal rotation was introduced for all elective functions, with the exception of the presidency to which Tito was unanimously elected for the fourth time by a new type of parliament. Already past the age of seventy, he was beginning to withdraw from the day-to-day running of business, while keeping in his personal prerogative world affairs and the prestige of Communist Yugoslavia, seconded by Kardelj and Ranković. The Eighth Congress, which followed in 1965, was undramatic.

Freed from a completely centralised command, the economy had been turned over to the partial control of a decentralised political power. Regional economic and political rivalries turned for support to existing national feelings, which flowed into these new moulds. Yugoslavism had to retreat again under pressure from local leaderships. Nationality came to be associated more closely with locality, and caused divisions within the Party that cut across those between reformists and conservatives.

Meanwhile the economy continued to produce beyond its means, with a quickened pace of inflation, and foreign debts amounting by 1965 to over $1,000 million. The point was reached where the government feared that aid could actually come to an end, and it returned to economic reform. Backed by assistance, the 1965 reforms broke the back of centralised state control over the economy, gave up discrimination against private smallholders, slashed into unproductive personnel, cut back the share of investment in the national income, and led to the fall of another of Tito's trusted lieutenants. Ranković's disgrace in 1966 hit the coalition of all those who impeded economic change, and provided a scapegoat for all the previous failures.

In the turmoil that followed Ranković's fall, much less was heard of economic change, even though it had led to his disgrace, and had been more real than the much-vaunted political change. The new economic policy was being applied by a personnel unchanged but for Ranković and his police supporters. Investment began to rise sharply, and prices resumed their upward trend along with unemployment, which had been rising steadily since the early 1950s. No longer able to provide jobs at home, the government removed restrictions on the right to seek employment abroad, and it abolished visas to encourage tourism. Free movement in and out of Yugoslavia was thus virtually allowed from the mid-1960s. As far as travel was concerned, Yugoslavia became an open country. The age-old rural problem was on the way to being really solved, not by collectivisation and industrialisation, but through industrialisation and emigration – a line that the parliamentary government of the 1920s had tried to follow.

Non-alignment remained the established basis of Yugoslavia's foreign policy, even though her economic weakness prevented her influence from being anything but superficial. Tito's initial disappointment and fears when Khrushchev had to step down in 1964 were eventually allayed, as his visit to Moscow in 1965 and Brezhnev's to Belgrade the following year reaffirmed Yugoslavia's special relationship with the Soviet Union. That was even before the military take-over in Athens and the Israeli victory in 1967 made the Yugoslav president dread a change in the Near Eastern balance of power which could threaten his own regime. The tone of public pronouncements became openly anti-Western, and the cause of Communism in Yugoslavia was made to appear as being still in its revolutionary phase, facing numerous enemies within and without.

In the absence of a fully open and rational discussion of the real issues to be faced and of the real choices available, the changes brought about by modernisation were taking place, not only in a very serious economic situation, but also in an even more fragmented political and social system. Although it still effectively prevented any coming together of people outside it, the Party was so divided within itself that it was no longer clear what it was trying to do. It had ceased to be much of an organisational whole since it had developed into a plurality of regional leagues, most of which had jumped on to the back of the nationalist band-wagon. The problems of economic reorganisation, management efficiency, links with Europe, constitutional arrangements, and national identity, merged into political problems. In place of solutions, mere words were repeated to an apathetic public. Authority was being challenged by local Communist groups and nationalisms, churches and intellectuals, workers and students, to which one should add violent strikes, increased criminality, general hooliganism, and rampant corruption. It was acknowledged that anti-Communism was spreading. The ideology of the ruling class no longer satisfied even its own children.

The student revolt of the summer of 1968 and its reverberations presented the Party apparatus with its most serious domestic challenge since it had come to power – more serious even than the contained subversion of the so-called 'Cominformists' two decades earlier. It showed that, when all the grievances came to a head rather than coalesced, the people at the top found themselves united by the simple reflex of the preservation of their power. Theirs was still the organisation and the ability to manoeuvre within and around the opposition trends, which were confused, disorganised and not consciously synchronised.

Domestic and foreign events had come together again. The Yugoslav leadership had supported the reforms in Czechoslovakia as being in the best interest of socialism, but it had taken care to advise the Communist leaders in that country on how far they could safely go. But because of his faith in Soviet Communism, Tito was apt to misread the intentions of the Kremlin, and the Czechoslovak crisis of 1968 for a while again worsened relations with the Soviet Union. The Belgrade government condemned the Soviet military intervention in Czechoslovakia as a serious blow against socialism; it proclaimed Yugoslavia's determination to defend her independence; and with the formulation of the 'Brezhnev doctrine' of the limited sovereignty of socialist states, it looked anew to the West to provide serious cover. NATO and the United States gave warning signals to deter the Soviet Union from any move against Yugoslavia.

The Soviet danger was put to good use to defend the regime's domestic position, but it soon appeared that both sides were anxious to avoid a breach. In order to check the advance of non-Communist influences in the country, the Yugoslav leadership not only quickly restored working relations with its Soviet counterpart, but turned to a normalisation of relations with the whole Communist world – China and Albania included. At the same time it was anxious to cultivate the goodwill of the West. It finally settled down to good-neighbour relations with Italy, based unashamedly on mutual interest, and then turned to the rest of the European Economic Community. Since it was obviously in Yugoslavia's interest to be on good terms with the other Communist countries as well as with the West, non-alignment remained the only foreign policy acceptable to all trends of its ruling League of Communists, but, as interpreted by Tito, it was both a diplomacy of prestige and a contribution to the propagation of socialism. Under her leader, who tried to be the guide of a movement of uncommitted states, Yugoslavia in the late 1960s increasingly looked to the West culturally and economically, while remaining tied to the East ideologically. Her foreign policy was a compound of megalomaniac tendencies, ideological inclinations, political necessities, economic realities and reflexes of fear.

After the great fear of 1968 had been overcome, a Ninth Congress was held in March 1969 to restore the balance between economic reforms and Party authority. With a sense of having Western support against the Soviet threat, a fragile unity of Party line and public opinion had been achieved again. A series of stop-gap measures, blending concessions and threats, had managed to restore a modicum of calm. The new line was to hold the system together, with the old Stalinist technique of treating as all alike those who disapproved of socialist Yugoslavia as it then stood.

Tito's personal involvement in all fields greatly increased again. Aged seventy-seven in 1969, he gathered his energy to act the part of inspirer, helmsman, father, guide and commander, and to ensure that power should be located in the Party. He went on extensive tours of the country, to put across the newly-hardened ideological line, and in 1970 on a tour of Africa and the European Economic Community. More than ever before, the regime and the country were linked to his person. Reforms came to an end, except for the continued constitutional implementation of greater autonomy both for the republics and for Serbia's associated provinces, as a counterpart to reinforced Party unity. To check the growing tendency to ethnocentrism, there was a renewed campaign against nationalism, with the emphasis on the association between common state, League of Communists and Tito.

The slogans were all about 'Yugoslav socialist patriotism' and 'Tito's

Yugoslavia'. Such propaganda merely ensured that emotional nationalism would wax extravagant, particularly in Croatia and in Serbia. In Serbia, nationalism reacted against the trend towards the sovereignty of the individual federated territories, a trend that left over 42 per cent of Serbs stranded in other areas, yet still branded as defenders of centralism. In Croatia, nationalism reacted against unitarism in any form, and these attempts to stimulate anew some Yugoslavism played their part in the rise of the national movement in Croatia between 1968 and 1971.

By 1970 it seemed that economic reforms had achieved little beyond devolving misinvestment to regional and local government. The balance of payments fell short by $125 million, and the situation was particularly serious in that it coincided with the preparation of a new five-year plan which would finally bring to an end the role of the state as an accumulator of investment resources. Anxious to prevent social and political conflicts, the government decided to give top priority to finding ways of 'stabilising' the economy, and to leave the plan until after that had been achieved. Politicians were told to reveal the full truth about the economy, so as to be able to obtain public consent for measures which were bound to be unpopular.

'Fin de partie'

The confused and heterogeneous, but spontaneous, awakening introduced by the reformist wave of 1965 had culminated in 1968. Certain forces in the trade unions, in the new generation that was taking over some of the regional executives, and generally in university youth, seemed to be groping towards a broad consensus – to free intellectual and artistic creation, and to remove the concepts of 'class' and 'nation' from their faded stereotypes. There had appeared to be a certain complicity between those politicians in Croatia who stood up for the rights of their nation, and their counterparts in Serbia who saw in such a trend a contributory factor to their own quest for democratisation. The fear of a groundswell, coinciding with external events, brought the central leadership to react with Tito's full authority in 1971–2. The political élite was cleansed of all those who had acquired a genuine, popular audience, and who were accused of nationalism, liberalism and technocratism.

The ship of state was put back on course by a policy symbolised in 1974 by yet another constitution with its 406 clauses (it set up a world record) and by the Tenth Congress (an apotheosis of President Tito). The pressure for reforms was ritualised through continued decentralisation, so much so that the new constitution almost turned the Yugoslav federation into an eight-unit confederation, thus damaging the very basis of the Communists' restoration of the Yugoslav union, which had been conceived as a federation of equal nations, and not as a coming together of pre-existing 'states'. All this was done, however, under the vigilant eye of a redisciplined Party whose 'democratic centralism' was to be honoured and practised again. President Tito's action did restore order – in the League of Communists, in the press, in the universities, and in the world of culture in general. He had intervened dazzlingly to maintain the foundations of Communism such as they had been instilled into him in his youth, but at the price of precipitating the decline in the prestige of the ruling party. The purges had been carried out by relying on alliances with and within the various local leaderships, and they had left the League shorn of many of its most prominent personalities. Thereafter the aged president worked at preparing his succession through the implementation of a collective leadership – which was the theme of the Eleventh Congress, in 1978. This was intended both to prevent a struggle for the succession, and anyone ever again wielding such power as he had – in order to keep his achievements and his memory intact and unique.

The last decade of the reign had an unreal appearance. At last proclaimed life president in 1974 at eighty-two after seven successive terms, Tito spent most of his time in solitary luxury, far from the capital, in his island, mountain or country retreats, on royal visitations or foreign travel. He indulged in the megalomania of the aging despot, basking in the ever-growing cult of his personality. His paternalism enabled him to discipline Party cadres without losing their support, and his popularity at large to take unpopular decisions. In order to restore ideological order, he had pointed to the armed forces as the bastion, not only of the country's independence, but of its social and political order as well. The army had become a political actor. Created by the Communist Party, it remained the armed force of the League of Communists, but it also became something of an extended praetorian guard.

In order to restore ideological order, Tito had also left credit and investment decisions to local Party leaders, which enabled these to satisfy their regional bases. Encouraged by the political reaction against 'techno-managerial' forces, massive government intervention had started again. Obviously, it was decentralised, or rather polycentralised,

with each region going about building its own capacities. Decentralisation so conceived had strengthened what Djilas called the 'feuda-
lisation' of Yugoslavia, producing eight little party-states with eight
competing economies. Altogether, they produced more than they
earned, imported increasing quantities of the raw materials needed for
their industries, and left their own mineral and agricultural resources
unexploited. When the international slowdown after 1973 intensified
the problems caused by Yugoslavia's 'overheated' economy, bad
harvests being thrown in for good measure, the balance of payments
deficit in 1979 attained $3,400 million. And yet that was when Tito
chose to uphold his country as a model to no less a forum than the
Assembly of the International Monetary Fund meeting in Belgrade.
Deficit and debt for the insufficiently developed, he said, ensured
equality between regions, whatever the degree of development; as the
Yugoslav economy was balanced, so should the world economy be
balanced.

The Yugoslav president had always played for the big stakes, first in
the Communist movement, and then in the non-aligned movement. The
latter having to all intents and purposes collapsed in the mid-1970s, it is
possible to read in the policy of Tito's last years the ultimate ambition of
negotiating between Moscow and Peking. Without compromising his
country's independence, he had entered into a close relationship with the
Soviet Union. Yugoslavia's non-alignment had never been a plain refusal
to align. It could even be said that it had been more of a hybrid alignment, and yet it had allowed her to act as a link between the two blocs.
The need for such a link no longer existed, and she was returning once
again to the drabber 'grey' area it had been agreed she belonged to in the
later stages of the Second World War. During its last decade, Titoism
had anyhow already run its course, and it had gone back on what were
seen by most Yugoslavs as the genuine advances of the 1960s. Kardelj's
death in 1979 had removed the last of the lieutenants. If the system in
that last decade still appeared to solve the country's problems, it was by a
mixture of magic, pretentiousness, consumerism, corruption and
foreign loans.

When Tito died on 4 May 1980, a few days before his eighty-eighth
birthday, the unease felt by average Yugoslavs stemmed from the fear
that their way of life might be disturbed. Tito, for them, had become
over the years the symbol of a Yugoslav style that had less to do with
socialism, self-management and non-alignment, than with freedom of
movement, the advent of the consumer society, and fending for oneself.

There was both fear and hope in the unknown to come. In the years that preceded Tito's death, the country had experienced such stagnation in government that in the vacuum that followed, the successors delayed the extensive economic innovations which necessity demanded. They dared no more than return to measures aimed at curtailing investment, raising exports and containing the rise in nominal incomes, with the usual devaluation that accompanied every economic reform since 1952.

Yugoslavia was facing the full onslaught of an acute economic and financial crisis, the result of misconceived ideological planification, investomania, and the squandering of foreign credits and remittances, all of which were exacerbated by bad harvests and by the rising price of oil. A decade of overheated growth dependent on foreign credits – when investment had come to represent 40 per cent of the gross national product, when outside capital is estimated to have contributed a quarter of gross investment, and when republics had come to control their own borrowings – had ended. The climax of real wages had been reached in 1978. By the end of 1981, with the country's hard-currency obligations running at $20,000 million (compared to Poland's $27,000 and Brazil's $86,000 million), and inflation around 50 per cent, living standards had begun to decline.

The flow of capital in the 1960s and 1970s had generally exasperated the contradictions of Eastern European economies. Yugoslavia, in particular, had become accustomed to the ready availability of international finance which enabled her to pay debts with new debts, and thus go on 'muddling through', but Western creditors were now indicating their reluctance to pay more. The old consensus in favour of large-scale aid was coming to an end, and the new emphasis was on getting developing countries to put their houses in order before more was done for them. Whereas in 1979 Tito had lectured the International Monetary Fund (to which his country had an accumulated debt of $2,500 million) on Yugoslavia as model to the world, by 1983 it was the director-general of that same organisation who denounced at the United Nations Conference on Trade and Development (UNCTAD) meeting in Belgrade the laxist financial policy followed by too many developing nations.

With enormous difficulties, Yugoslavia met the 1982 $4,800 million debt schedule, and she prepared to face the higher figure of $5,300 million for 1982, firmly set against re-scheduling, for prestige reasons, even though several badly indebted countries had already welcomed it. The IMF and the United States nevertheless rallied support. After a long negotiation, an international rescue operation was mounted, presented as a package of credits ($5,000 million) to restore Yugoslavia's immediate solvency, and to help her carry out her austerity programme. Face was saved in so far as the Belgrade government could take it publicly as a vote of confidence, even though it knew it to be really a motion of concern. In return for it, in the summer of 1983 it issued its long-awaited 'stabilisation programme', intended to go back to the abandoned reforms of 1965, to shock the economy out of its stagnation through a cooling therapy, and to bring painful changes to the life of every citizen. The party was over.

Most observers admitted at last that the economic crisis was structural rather than temporary, but the political crisis was even more serious. The reforms in the economy had constantly been frozen by political constraints which, in Yugoslavia and since Stalin's death, could hardly be said to have been imposed by Moscow. Development since Tito's death had strengthened the assertiveness of regional structures, as the policy of the central leadership had continued to balance ethnic groups and federal units against each other, playing on the 'peripheral' ones to weaken the 'core' of Serbs and Croats. This had left the Croats more bitter than ever against Belgrade; it had led to the explosion of Albanian nationalism in the province of Kosovo in 1981; it had stimulated an emotional reaction among Serbs; and it had brought to the surface an Islamic assertion in Bosnia and Herzegovina. The voluble self-criticism that appeared after Tito's death soon grew to question the validity of a self-management that provided no more than a veil of legitimacy. The dissatisfaction of the élites, the emergence of an intellectual proletariat, growing popular disenchantment, a general decline in confidence, all pointed to a crisis of legitimacy.

The ruling class had been granted territorial shares of sovereignty in recognition for services rendered. These were no longer relevant, and the monarch was dead. The government that he had left behind had run out of ideas. There was a substantial trend in the League of Communists favouring some overhaul of the system. This was felt at the Twelfth Congress in 1982 where deep divisions at the top were not far from erupting, but in the end no one was brave enough to ask for structural changes, and unanimity hovered around the lowest common denominator – the legitimising slogans ('And after Tito – Tito!' or 'Our socialist, federal, self-managing, independent and non-aligned fatherland – Tito's Yugoslavia'). The opening up of the press was a sign of the Party's weakness, not of a new policy. Tito was no longer there to impose a consensus over a divided Party. There were heated discussions about a number of important issues of recent history, dozens of open petitions and protests by intellectuals as well as questions about Tito's legacy and how to tackle it.

The first signs of de-Titoisation were in the air. Not only was there a good deal of it in the day-to-day running of diplomacy and in economic statements, but books appeared which implicitly reduced Tito's stature, and demystified the standard accounts of the all-heroic partisan war. The government had not said openly that the austerity programme had been imposed by Yugoslavia's creditors; some people were already saying that it would not have happened under Tito. The successors were probably not sorry to shed some of their burden of problems back to yesterday's hero, but in so doing they were allowing the regime's essential claims to legitimacy to be questioned.

The end of Tito's way

Tito's face was still to be seen everywhere, public obeisance was still made at his tomb in the 'House of Flowers', and public criticism of him still remained unacceptable, but it was increasingly felt that the appeals to continue treading the late leader's path were now being superseded by the situation. Tito was a historic personality: he belonged to the past. The present was in a state of paralysis, and the late leader was to a great extent responsible for it. Paralysed by the contradictions between a power structure that remained, however loosely, modelled on the East, and an economy that contained a free market, however undeveloped, the system was becoming synonymous with mismanagement. Yugoslav economists were challenging self-management itself as being essentially conservative in the worst sense of the word, and responsible for a situation where the country found itself once again, as before the revolution, near the bottom of the European economic league-table.

In 1983, in order to avoid bankruptcy – for she could no longer pay back her debts because she could no longer borrow – Yugoslavia had to accept what was in fact IMF control. In return for a salvage plan, the government had taken certain undertakings, in particular concerning prices, interest rates and exchanges, and some of this had been translated into legislation after long and fierce debates – notably to give the National Bank control over the management of all debts and credits. The legislation passed did not, however, contain a clear plan to implement the much-needed restructuring, in spite of pressing government calls for unity around such a programme, and 1983 failed to achieve the desired effect. Yet priority had been given to exports at the expense of the standard of living, and the unlocking of prices had pushed inflation up. A price freeze was introduced again at the beginning of 1984, and the government went back to the IMF.

Inflation by the middle of that year had officially reached the European record of 62 per cent; the standard of living had fallen by over 30 per cent since the beginning of the decade; unemployment was over 15 per cent of the workforce, with more than half the unemployed aged under twenty-four, and additional concealed unemployment in the social sector (in spite of between 600,000 and one million Yugoslavs employed abroad); the debt schedule was nearer $6,000 million; the total hard currency debt had increased to $21,000 million. A new agreement was reached with the IMF which laid down the law for receiving further credits and a nine-year re-scheduling. There were more draconian measures, half of the industrial output was freed from price control, more was to come, and the Yugoslavs tightened their belts further.

How did they do it? The situation was one of crisis, but it did not appear catastrophic. Although the number of strikes in 1984 was considerably higher than in previous years, social stability had not yet been imperilled. For a start, people had become accustomed since 1980 to living in a state of economic crisis, with high inflation and unemployment. Their recent peasant past still enabled them to hold out. Even when they lived in towns, most of them still had either a smallholding or a relative on the land who provided food. Many had a bank account in foreign currency, either abroad or in Yugoslavia (which was not only legal but encouraged), or a relative working in the West who could send marks, francs or dollars. The extended family acted as a shock-absorber. With official working hours in the social sector starting early and ending early, with an effective working day estimated (as published by *Borba* on 19 March 1984) to be no more than 4 hours 9 minutes, there was time for overtime, second jobs, and a full-blown 'black economy'. Such factors of resilience did not appear in statistics, and help to explain the endurance of a society that otherwise seemed to have been put into abeyance. Other factors included an attitude of defeatism, a realisation that the party was over, but also a continued conviction that the West would bail them out eventually. In the meantime, it was a question of lying low and surviving.

At the end of 1984, the federal authorities were admitting that the anti-inflationary plan, adopted in 1980, was still being implemented only very partially. It was coming up against tough resistance from the Party bureaucracy, which was firmly entrenched in the regional adminis-trations. Real power was in the hands of republican and provincial oligarchies who had been taking significant economic decisions that were not based on economic criteria, and with few economic qualifications. These had gone unchecked since there were no channels for political criticism, and no sanctions against political mistakes. The system had become one of regional power structures defending their vested interests, competing between themselves, and uniting only in the defence of their general hold on the reins of power. Public criticism of the politicians surfaced to the point where newspapers carried articles saying that there could be no serious economic reform without a democratisation of the electoral system, and that what was needed was a new political generation free from ideological prejudice or nationalistic passion. The outgoing prime minister is on record as saying, in the spring of 1984: 'Either our political system will be made to work, or we shall be under pressure to have it changed.'

Pressure indeed there was. Disillusioned Yugoslavs were deserting the Party in droves, from workers who did so in silence to prestigious members who were open in their disappointment. Anti-Communist sentiments surfaced publicly, with calls for real democracy, and pluralism – coming from the Party itself, from retired partisan cadres of the People's Liberation War and even more so from intellectuals. Freed from fear, dissidents came to life in 1984 – journalists, poets, novelists, artists, sociologists – to contest the idea that the League of Communists was the only political institution capable of rising above individual interests. Although the climate differed from republic to republic, being most open in Belgrade and in Ljubljana, more and more people distanced themselves from a system which was seen to be decayed, divided, and incapable of solving anything, let alone economic problems.

The rotation that year installed a new government team of younger individuals coming from their respective regional bureaucracies with a reputation for toughness. Their neo-conservative trend found immediate support among the military – almost the only centralised institution left in the state – but it was difficult for them to consolidate it, since any change was bound to provoke defiance in some other coalition of groups and republics. All they could do was react nervously to the challenge, by harassing the critical intellectuals. There was a series of arrests followed by clamorous and unproductive trials which provoked a great show of solidarity. A few foreign journalists were expelled – including Nora Beloff, then completing her controversial study, *Tito's Flawed Legacy*. Amnesty International was to report in 1985 that between 1980 and 1984 more than 500 people a year had been sentenced for political transgressions, mostly 'verbal offences'. In the words of a leader-writer in *Le Monde* (27 April), the Yugoslav authorities seemed to be wanting to 'shut up words at the time when they were freeing prices'.

The year 1984 was not an Orwellian one for Yugoslavia. It was the year when the emperor was seen to be naked, when the myths began to crumble, when people began to want to know how they had come to be in such a situation. A crisis had come out into the open which was at one and the same time a crisis of post-totalitarianism, of transfer to modernity, and of national identity. It was not really new, but it was now seen for what it was – a crisis of the system that had been symbolised by Tito. 1984 was the year when 'Tito's way' came to an end without anyone saying it in so many words, when his island retreat was turned into a national park, and when his luxury yacht was put up for sale.

3

THE 'GASTARBEITER' WHO BECAME
A PHARAOH – JOSIP BROZ TITO

The emigrant and the conspirator

The Tito era (1945–80) takes up exactly half of Yugoslavia's history so far – thirty-five years out of seventy – but it already belongs to the past. Before it there were twenty-three years of monarchy – parliamentary, then authoritarian, finally semi-authoritarian and pseudo-parliamentary – and the cruel interval of the Second World War. Since then, the country has gradually moved to post-Titoism, after an initial period where its political establishment pretended that the dead leader's spirit still led them on. It needed the then French prime minister, Raymond Barre, to state the obvious, in Belgrade, six months after Tito's death, on 14 November 1980: 'Yugoslavia existed before Tito, and Yugoslavia will exist after Tito.'

We are now at a sufficient distance from Tito to see him whole. Historians can study him in the light of new books that have appeared, and of archives, most often at second hand, but occasionally at first hand. Hundreds of books have appeared in Yugoslavia on Tito, particularly in 1980–4. Most of them tell us more about his posthumous cult than about his historical character. There have, however, been interesting exceptions, which will be looked at in Chapter 9. Milovan Djilas's important *Tito: the Story from Inside* (1981), published outside Yugoslavia, should be mentioned here, and so, in a completely different vein, should the significantly titled 'Yugoslavia after Tito', written by an influential Croatian Communist, and published in Zagreb in 1986 (Dušan Bilandžić, *Jugoslavija posle Tita, 1980–1985*).

It is now possible to see that Tito's motive power was his ambition. Right from the start, his aim was to move up in the world. His national environment could never satisfy his desires. The young peasant Josip Broz left his native village of Kumrovec and his province of Croatia to seek a better living and a higher social status in Vienna, just as later, once he had become leader of Yugoslavia, Marshal Tito would not rest content with that platform. He sought to play bigger parts on the more prestigious stages of international Communism and of the non-aligned movement. At the age of nineteen, he went off to build a new life for himself in the capital of the Austro-Hungarian Monarchy, dreaming of becoming an engineer. (That was the disguise he would later adopt as a conspirator.) His ambition made him move with ease from a rural South Slav environment, to the German industrial milieu of Vienna, then to the military until the collapse of Austria-Hungary. He worked for a while in the Daimler works before enlisting as an army technician, and eventually going through a school for non-commissioned officers. A loyal NCO of the Habsburg emperor's army, he was awarded medals for his services both in peacetime and during the Great War. He took part in the invasion of Serbia in 1914 (this was a long-kept state secret) before going on to fight on the Eastern Front.

He did not, like so many of his Slav compatriots in the Austro-Hungarian forces, surrender or go over to the enemy, and he was wounded when the Russians captured him. Even when he had recovered, he did not enrol in the volunteers which were being recruited among Yugoslav prisoners of war, nor was he quick to join the Bolsheviks. In Russia in 1917, in the middle of the revolution, he actually toyed for a while with the idea of emigrating to the United States. When he revealed this in one of his televised monologues on his youth, in the spring of 1976, President Tito added half jokingly: 'Had I done it, I would have become a millionaire'. This could indicate that personal ambition led to revolutionary zeal rather than the other way round. In fact it was not until late in 1919 that Tito joined the Communists, at a time when Austria-Hungary was dead and buried.

When he returned home in 1920 to the unified Kingdom of the Serbs, Croats and Slovenes, it was as a virtual foreigner in his native land, to start yet a new career as a clandestine revolutionary. He was already at the head of the Zagreb Communist Party organization when he was arrested in 1928, tried and sentenced to a five-year prison term. On his release, he was admitted to the Central Committee, and then to the Politbureau, of the Communist Party of Yugoslavia, and went to work for the apparatus of the Comintern in Moscow. His years in detention were certainly not useless to him. They may well have saved him from sharing the fate of some of the other leading Yugoslav Communists who were purged in that period. They certainly made a better Communist of him, for he was able to read, study and indulge in political discussions while in the prisons of the old regime. The way was open which was to lead him to the top of his country's Communist Party.

In Moscow, Tito appears to have been a fervent yet shrewd

representative of an insignificant party that was in crisis, and in whose weakened émigré leadership the role of intellectuals was coming to an end. What was his attitude at the time of the liquidation of the Yugoslav Communist old guard? All that one can say for sure is that he survived and was promoted, while most of his compatriots in Moscow perished in Stalin's purges. At the end of 1937, he had made it: he was first secretary of the Communist Party of Yugoslavia. Back in Yugoslavia in 1936, Tito was to return often to Moscow up till the outbreak of war. Hand-picked after a long selection process and an exhaustive investigation, the new leader of the Yugoslav Party seemed to be exactly what Stalin looked for. The perfect conspirator and organiser, he would show uncompromising determination in selecting an unwavering team of lieu-tenants, and in building up an active underground apparatus of militants. There is no doubt that it was a Stalinist who had been chosen to take over the Yugoslav Party at the time of the purges.

Both the Austrian and the Russian factor had been important in moulding Tito's personality. He had not been one of those young revolutionaries who had wanted to blow up the old Habsburg dynastic conglomerate in the name of the nationalist ideal of South Slav unity. He had been influenced by the concept of a multinational state whose subjects owed loyalty to a polity that transcended their region, their linguistic group or their ethnic community. A relative latecomer to Communism, he had learnt in Russia that institutions mattered more than ideals in acquiring and keeping power, even though ideology was important as a cement for those institutions.

Tito set to work early in 1938. He purged and reorganised the Communist network throughout Yugoslavia, and soon had a unified party around him, responding to his lead. He brought to the fore a group of new men who owed nothing to the old Communists and who believed in the necessity of strong leadership to keep party unity and purity. He applied Stalin's successive tactical moves until the German invasion: neutrality in the imperialists' war; strikes in the ordnance factories, some co-operation with separatist movements (even with the German ethnic community), and demonstrations against the call-up; eventually, where it was deemed necessary, jumping on to the patriotic bandwagon. That generation of Yugoslav Communists was committed body and soul to the Soviet Union and to Stalin. The Soviet Union was the fatherland of socialism, and it was also the land of the Russians, for whom many Yugoslavs had a feeling of Slav affection.

In 1941 Hitler attacked Yugoslavia in the spring, and the Soviet

Union in the summer. It was then that Tito issued his call to arms. In doing so, he was obviously responding to an appeal by the Comintern to assist Russia in resisting the German invasion; but he was also seizing the opportunity provided by the war to launch the revolution. Officially called the People's Liberation War, the Communist-led struggle in occupied and partitioned Yugoslavia is at times described as a patriotic enterprise against foreign occupation troops and their native auxiliaries, at other times as a revolutionary undertaking against the forces of domestic and international reaction. In another of his television reminiscences, in the spring of 1972, Tito acknowledged that 'it was well and truly a civil war, but we did not want to admit it at the time, because it would have been detrimental to our cause.'

The insurgent and the revolutionary

It should not be forgotten that the history of the Second World War in Yugoslavia has, in general, been written from the point of view of the winning side in the civil war, and that the survival of records there has been left to the tender mercies of the legitimising selection of official criteria, quite apart from the hazards of war and revolution. Nevertheless, as will be seen in Chapter 9, with the passing of time and the availability of source-material outside Yugoslavia, some sense of historical perspective has begun to emerge. The myths are gradually giving way to a messy tale of internecine strife, where insurrection was an act of hope or of hopelessness, and where most people's worry, most of the time, was how to survive.

Even for the guerrilas, to survive and then to eliminate domestic opponents was more important than to fight foreign occupation troops. Insurgency was efficient to the point of destroying the possible implementation of a long-term Axis plan of action for the whole area, and of bogging down important enemy forces. But the fact of civil war also allowed Germany and Italy, which could not afford to have an excessive number of troops in Yugoslavia, to keep them at acceptable levels. The tension between the two main occupying powers, added to the relatively limited number of their forces, in turn enabled the insurgency, and the civil war, to thrive.

Yugoslavs were slaughtered by other Yugoslavs more than by foreign soldiers. Once the 'others' had been assigned the role of vermin, it was no longer wrong to eliminate them, all the more so because it was necessary to remove those who stood in the way of one's designs. The guerillas would have removed even more of their compatriots, in the name of their infallible truth, or for the sake of their country's future happiness, had they not been held back by the Germans, whom they hated, and even more so by the Italians, whom they despised – not to mention the fear of what their outside protectors in the East or in the West would think of them. They were all resourceful and tenacious. They were often dispersed, even defeated, but they could not be destroyed. They neither gave nor expected any quarter. They were double-faced and even multi-faced. They indulged in what has since been called 'parallel action' against other insurgents – attacking them when they were already in action against foreign troops. They negotiated with the enemy to obtain time, food, medicines, weapons, prisoner exchanges, local ceasefires, and more. At the same time, no territory controlled by German or Italian divisions was ever lost. 'Liberated' territories were no-man's-land, or localities whose evacuation had been decided in advance and higher up, or taken over from each other and from the Ustashas.

In waging its revolutionary struggle, the Communist-led People's Liberation Movement under Tito set up contacts with all sorts of people, wherever these contacts could be of use – with separatists of one kind or another, with insurgents of royalist allegiance under General Mihailović's command, with other more or less autonomous nationalist chetnik fighters, with Italians or Germans at various command levels. Hard pressed by the increasing tightness of the Axis ring closing in on him in the spring of 1943, Tito used existing prisoner-exchange contacts in order to approach the German command in Zagreb. He sent a high-level delegation, made up of Milovan Djilas (who was to become vice-president before falling from grace, going to prison and turning into the father of Yugoslavia's political dissidence), Koča Popović (one-time poet, future chief of the General Staff and secretary of state for foreign affairs) and Vladimir Velebit (son of a pre-war general and future ambassador to London) with the purpose of arranging a ceasefire.

After having stated in writing that their main enemies were the chetniks and not the Germans, they offered to stop harrassing Axis forces if the partisans were allowed to return to their homes, or to go East and fight the chetniks. These they denounced to the Germans as being both tolerated by the Italians and connected to the British. The possibility was also envisaged of joint defensive action of partisans and Germans in case of an Anglo-American landing. Tito's representatives did not shrink from telling the German generals that they would fight the British, for they really believed they would have to do it if the British landed and went on to give support to the partisans' rivals, the chetniks, who would then all rally to Mihailović's command. They did not, however, say that their real objective was to penetrate Mihailović's territory. For strategic reasons, the Germans were most sensitive about what was happening in Serbia, where the population was strongly opposed to them, and Mihailovićist in allegiance.

Naturally enough, Tito also did not want the Russians to know that anything more important than the exchange of prisoners had been discussed. During the negotiations, the Germans called a halt to their anti-partisan drive, while Tito suspended guerilla operations on the Zagreb-Belgrade railway line. This made it easier for him to win a difficult victory over local chetnik contingents, who were moving from Montenegro into Herzegovina to block the way to the partisans. Then, when the talks with the Germans came to a halt, Tito was still making overtures to chetnik commanders in that area where Bosnia, Herzegovina and Montengro meet (an entangled and sensitive area from all points of view – geographic, ethnic, political), in order to detach them from Mihailović. Harassed as they were by both Germans and partisans, these captains were also going through difficult times.*

The reasons why the Communists eventually came out on top are relatively simple. Tito's movement, which had been almost destroyed in eastern Yugoslavia in 1941, was able to emerge again like a phoenix from its ashes by penetrating the desperate struggle started by the Orthodox Serbs to survive the 'final solution' attempted by the Fascist Ustasha regime of the satellite state of Croatia. The movement then developed by thriving on the anarchy of that pseudo-state, as the Croats themselves turned away from it. With the collapse of Italy, most of those who wanted to find themselves on the side of the Allies in what had been the Italian occupation zone threw in their lot with the partisans. The Communists, under Tito's direction, quickly established an overall unity of strategy which enabled them to exploit situations, and practise a variety of tactics, while showing a bold, single, face to the world outside. There was no such unity of purpose among the anti-Communists, who were never able to co-ordinate their efforts.

Only as leader of a patriotic resistance could Tito hope to retain the support of non-Communist followers and combatants, but the primary

* For the literature on the 1943 negotiations, see chapter 9, note, pp. 140–2.

and long-term aim of the Yugoslav Communist leadership was the conquest of power. The concept of 'national liberation' was thus used as an instrument of social revolution and political conquest in the course of the civil war that raged under multiple foreign occupation. A physically terrorised, economically deprived and politically naïve peasantry supplied the manpower for that operation.

Some of the military aspects of Tito's war leadership now appear dubious, to say the least, but he had the ability always to recover quickly, while his supreme gift was his political insight. Without contradiction or hypocrisy, he tied a popular resistance movement to the cause of world Communism led by the Soviet Union. In the course of the struggle against both foreign occupation forces and native opponents, he forged a new power, and in so doing, did not distinguish between the revolutionary transformation of Yugoslav society and his personal ascendancy over it. By the time that he had to reach an understanding with the Allies over the shape of his country's government after the end of the war, he already held almost all the cards. He needed international recognition from the Powers, and he duly obtained it by making a few very temporary concessions of form in the agreement which he signed with King Peter's last prime minister. That agreement soon became worthless in so far as all the attempts at setting up some political opposition were curbed before the general elections, in spite of lip-service paid to formal pluralism in the People's Front led by the Communist Party. There followed the liquidation of all surviving political opponents, and the civil war eventually petered out in the 1950s.

In the West, Tito has made the fortune of several clichés. He has been called a 'born rebel', a 'pragmatist', an 'ideological innovator', a 'nationalist'. In fact, he was a born ruler, a born leader, in the full sense of the word, the Latin *dux*, of whom in the 1930s and '40s there were Mussolini in Italy, Hitler in Germany, Franco in Spain, Metaxas in Greece, Antonescu in Romania and Pavelić in Croatia. Tito's pragmatism was essentially tactical. He was a practical politician and a statesman concerned about his place in history. As for ideology, it was for him inseparable from politics. Far from being a thinker, he tended rather to be suspicious of ideological novelties: they could undermine his own achievement and power. At the same time, he was always quick to see the public-relations potential of some ideas, and he was ready to take advantage of other people's thinking. Just as he was no ideological innovator, so he was no nationalist. What he needed was a power-base and a sphere of action, so the Party and the state were all-important to him. It was his inseparable association with the state that eventually made him identify with the life of the nation, as interpreted by him.

The origin of his resistance to the Soviet leadership should also be sought in his love of power, and in his instinct of self-preservation. The conflict of 1948 was about power, not about ideology. Nevertheless, the clash with Stalin happened at a time when the People's Liberation Movement was still a live force to be reckoned with in Yugoslavia. That spirit underpinned Tito's resolve to maintain 'his' state and his position in it. The cult of Tito's personality, which was already well developed, served to strengthen Yugoslav resistance to Stalin. The role of the Party was increased, because it was the only source of legitimacy once Moscow had been removed, and because Party cadres linked their fate to Tito's towering authority.

Furthermore, Soviet claims were resisted with Soviet methods, and Tito fought back by adopting an even harsher Stalinist line. The leadership that he had selected and set up in the years before the Second World War remained, on the whole, united. Tito, however, who was essentially interested in the link with the Party apparatus, increasingly identified the Party with his person, and also placed himself above it, projecting his charismatic image to the country at large. A Leninist-Stalinist Party establishment, with a successful revolution behind it, a dominating leader at its head, and massive aid from the West to set it back on its feet, the Yugoslav regime came to be known as Titoism.

The superhuman ruler and the world statesman

Titoism was the consequence, not the cause, of the clash with Stalin. It was the result of the efforts made by a particular Party leadership to stay in power in spite of Stalin. Many things were to change in Yugoslavia after that crisis, but the central leadership never relinquished its monopoly of power, and Tito himself remained firmly at the helm until almost the very end, steering the regime this way and that according to the prevailing winds. By the force of things, it had become independent of the Soviet Union, and it had implemented different methods of development, but there were basic principles from which Tito never deviated, and limits beyond which he never went. In so far as it had acquired an originality of its own, Titoism was so closely limited to its domestic circumstances that it could hardly be transplanted. Otherwise it retained much in common with its original Soviet model. It may have encouraged Maoism, Hoxhism, Gomulkism, both Nagyism and Kadarism, Dubčekism, and even Ceausescuism, but they were all different intrinsically. As a specifically Yugoslav model, it was a myth – a heroic rendering of an historical reality, conceptualised and personalised.

Anti-Stalinism naturally opened the doors of the Communist Party of Yugoslavia to many deviations. Quite a number of its militants took the quarrel with Moscow to be a cue for more internal freedom. For reasons that were both political and economic, Tito had to give way to them on two occasions, first in the early 1950s, and then again in the late 1960s, but without ever making concessions on the question of the Party's monopoly of power. All sorts of allowances were made, on condition that the system itself were not questioned, and, as soon as he could, Tito would sort things out again and go back on course. He believed in the possibility of reconciliation with the Soviet Union after Stalin's death, and was eventually accepted on his own terms by Khrushchev – at a time when it was obvious to all that Moscow no longer enjoyed the world monopoly of ideological authority.

Even though the fall of Khrushchev deeply shocked him, and the invasion of Czechoslovakia put a heavy strain on his faith in the Soviet Union, Tito always managed to restore a working relationship with subsequent Soviet leaders. They could understand him. He was a man they could live with. His early experiences ensured that he would not fall over Westwards. Bilateral relations between Yugoslavia and the Soviet Union were rarely at stake. Rather it was international relations or the ups and downs of Third World countries that affected a reconciliation which was difficult to consummate but none the less, in the long run, lasting. Occasional divergences did not hinder the development of dialogue between the two countries – as Brezhnev and Tito rightly told us on the occasion of Tito's last pilgrimage to Moscow, in May 1979.

Tito did not see himself as the embodiment of defiance to the Soviet Union, in spite of the prestige he had acquired through the events which were later made to appear as a rebellion against Stalin. These anyway came to reinforce his earlier reputation as victorious leader of the partisans in their rebellion against Hitler. Tito saw himself as one of the leaders of international Communism, and wanted to be treated as such, because he considered that the success of the Yugoslav revolution entitled him to that status, because he could see that his tactics were subtler than those of the dictators in the Kremlin, and (last but certainly not least) because he wanted to build himself into an international figure.

His country by itself did not provide him with a big enough stage on which to play that part, and because the Communist world would not give him the role, he went to play it in the open-air theatre of the Third World. His government devoted much effort and spent much money on developing a progressive movement of non-aligned countries which he would lead. Yet all the time he retained a nostalgia for the socialist sphere. He cleverly used the West to protect him against pressure from Moscow, and he jockeyed for a leading position on the Communist front, ever on the look-out for chances to exert an influence on developments there, attempting to have the best of two, if not even of three, worlds.

The two dogmas of Titoism (called 'Tito's way' in Yugoslavia) were self-management and non-alignment, with the partisan war as the historic source of legitimacy and inspiration. Self-management, however, had come to cause more problems than it really solved, because it was accepted by Tito only to the extent that it would not interfere with fundamentals, and the fundamentals were concerned with political power. Tito wanted to be judged by his achievements as a world leader. The non-aligned movement did indeed play a certain part at a given moment on the international stage, as well as in Yugoslavia's diplomatic strategy, but it changed direction in the mid-1960s, and had disintegrated a decade later. Tito's endless journeying and summiting gratified his vanity and his taste for travel, but it is doubtful whether much remains to show for it. By the late 1970s, it certainly no longer corresponded to any deep Yugoslav yearning or interest. The Soviet intervention in Afghanistan did more to restore some measure of non-alignment among the non-aligned than all Tito's personal and itinerant diplomacy. If his final ambition in the last decade of his reign was to revitalise international Communism, this corresponded with his domestic policies in these years.

In his role as a world leader, Tito's initial catapult was Yugoslavia, which also restricted his sphere of action. Titoism had originally been taken up in the West as a contributory factor to the strategy of containment of Soviet power. It was regarded not as an isolated phenomenon, but as a precedent to be encouraged, one that would exploit the tension between the international Communist network and its centre in the Kremlin. It was seen as an eroding force which could not only contain the Soviet sphere, but actually reduce it. To Eastern Europe, Yugoslavia's importance lay in her capacity to deal on equal terms with the Soviet Union, and it was against possible Soviet aggression that the Western powers were anxious to bolster her up. Governments and public opinions were not otherwise much interested in Titoism.

Tito reigned for so long that he picked up all the accumulated myths of the history of the South Slavs. He certainly understood their importance in politics, and fostered many, but none so well as his own. Tito's was one of those authoritarian regimes that Western democracies favour so long as they provide apparent stability without too much pricking of decent liberal consciences. This applies particularly to Britain where nearly all tastes – anti-Communists, Russophobes, socialists of one tendency or another, various liberals, Thatcherite Tories, not to mention the faithful band of war-time admirers who range from pink to blue – have found something to savour in Titoism. This could be a split in the international Communist movement, a factor of destabilisation for Russia and her empire, a future for Communism, a lesson in survival, an air of continuity to British diplomacy, and other things besides. So much so that the cult of Tito seems to have survived better in Britain than in Yugoslavia.

Even so, who still remembers today the Marshal Tito Fellowship Fund of the School of Slavonic and East European Studies of the University of London, launched with fanfare and controversy at the end of 1980, or the 'Ode to Tito' by Malcolm Williamson, Master of the Queen's Musick, or Sir Fitzroy Maclean's consultancy for an epic film on Tito's life that never became a reality? Although it still crops up in official speeches, historians know that there was no continuity between British aid to the People's Liberation Movement in 1943–4 and the assistance supplied to Yugoslavia after 1948. The events of that year were an unforeseen gift from Clio which made it possible to present a coherent story of the solid and uninterrupted friendship between the United Kingdom and Communist Yugoslavia.

Tito's rule should be described as autocratic rather than totalitarian, for he was intent on controlling the immediate sources of power – the Party, along with the armed forces and the security forces. The rest concerned him much less, so that economy or culture could enjoy more or less autonomy. Changes did occur in these fields for as long as such developments did not threaten the continuity of political power, or – better still – in the degree to which they contributed to that continuity. However, these developments went so far that the period of the late 1960s can be seen as having come almost to the point of diluting Titoism. That is why Tito changed course again in 1971–2. Backed by the Army, he purged the Party, restored full control over the secret police, and his power was, once again, formally absolute.

The last years, nevertheless, had a surreal air to them. Tito was old and no longer in day-to-day control, yet these were 'his' years more than any earlier period. He had become the victim as well as the deity and high priest of the cult of his personality. The arrogance of Yugoslavia's non-alignment – which consisted in pontificating on every imaginable subject, making moral judgements on all possible issues, and giving advice to all foreign governments, but accepting only praise from the outside world – was part of Tito's policy of grandeur that had already shrunk. Attributing any crisis to super-power rivalry, it sheltered behind a non-aligned movement which had become too radical for Tito's liking, and where Yugoslavia's influence had much diminished. Living more than ever beyond its means, the regime could no longer afford its passion for big policy. To people at home, Titoism ran the risk of appearing to have been no more than a series of illusions performed by a ruling élite to retain power.

In what had always been fundamentally an authoritarian state of contradictions in equilibrium, Tito had become – depending on one's point of view – the charismatic leader who alone was able to conciliate all those contradictions, or the dead weight that blocked the way to all solutions.

Seven or eight months after Stalin's death, Tito is said by Djilas (*Sunday Times*, 11 May 1980) to have observed: 'It is incredible how quickly a man like that was forgotten.' Thoughts of immortality strengthened his determination to set off his personal power against impersonal institutions. He had always attached great importance to institutions, and he did not want a successor. The slogans after his death – 'What will there be after Tito? There will be Tito', 'After Tito – Tito' – were not just rhetoric. They corresponded to his wish. He wanted to be unique. He did not want anyone after him to be as powerful as he was, lest that other one should use such powers to dislodge the statue that he had been turned into. There would be no Tito II, and the memory of the one and only Tito would inspire the government machinery that he had set up. He put into place a collective leadership, which he saw as a transition to a leaderless mechanism of permanent musical chairs. There is an inevitable contrast between Tito's success and the fragility of his achievements.

'The optimists called him the first real Yugoslav; the pessimists called him the last one,' commented the *Guardian* (5 May 1980) at the time of Tito's death. This sounds good, but makes little sense in terms of history. At the time, readers could be forgiven for thinking they were reading something profound, whereas the words amounted to nothing more than a well-turned sentence for the editorial of a right-thinking paper the morning after a historic occasion. Tito was certainly not the first real Yugoslav. He was not the most idealistic Yugoslav; and were he to be the last, he would bear much of the blame for it. Yugoslavia is more than Tito, and the history of Yugoslavia does not boil down to the history of Tito, in spite of the role he has played in it.

The Yugoslav idea goes back to the 1830s, the state of Yugoslavia to 1918 and to a time when the Communists did not like it. The Communist Party of Yugoslavia contributed to the destruction of the Yugoslav state and then put it back together again in its own fashion. Tito's reign is now a chapter, albeit a long one, of Yugoslav history, and Yugoslavia lives on without him. She still lives with the legends that have accrued from a long and complex reign, with legends that have been generated, consciously and self-consciously, in Yugoslavia and abroad. Yugoslavia badly needs to look ahead; also, for the sake of perspective, and in order to know where she has come from and not get lost, she will occasionally have to look back further than Tito, and learn about her past. Now that the myths are beginning to be stripped away, the Yugoslavs themselves will soon be able to examine the dimensions of the man who led them for so long.

The Yugoslav revolution of which Tito was the leader, is an accomplished fact, with its new classes and its new social relationships. So is the federalism of its different regions and ethnic groups. By reuniting the Serbs and the Croats who had been set on each other by the Axis powers, and by granting the Macedonians the ethnic recognition which the monarchy had refused them, Tito's Communist regime gave a more solid foundation to Yugoslavia, even if it did not actually solve her national question. The country today has a pluralist society capped by the power of a monopolistic but feudalised Party leadership.

The regime inherited from Tito is both authoritarian and paralysed. Unity has been reinforced by dogma, by slogans, and by an apparatus that has wanted to force actual realities into predetermined and conceptualised stereotypes instead of trying to look closer at those realities and of working through them. There is a manner of thinking which believes that an independent, complex and united Yugoslavia can only survive if it does not have to liberalise her political structure. That view raises the question whether such a Yugoslavia is worth keeping. It is also countered by another manner of thinking according to which Yugoslavia can only live on, and develop, if she liberalises her system of government. Otherwise she risks not so much sudden death as insidious debilitation and multiple sclerosis, which will make it gradually more dependent on the Soviet Union again.

These contrasting views and the dilemma they pose are part of Tito's legacy to Yugoslavia.

4

TITOISM AND THE YUGOSLAV TRADITION

Realities and illusions

We know that no two Communist regimes are alike. Even though they all partake of the same nature, each has its distinctive features. The Titoist regime in Yugoslavia is, by general agreement, the most distinctive of all. It started off by standing out among the revolutionary regimes of Eastern Europe as the one that, in the immediate aftermath of the Second World War, went furthest on the way of autarkical Communism, copying the Stalinist model as closely as it could. Then, finding itself rejected as an outcast by its mentor, it was forced to adapt to its new situation, precariously balanced in a region of convergence and transition, where over the centuries outside influences have crossed and overlapped, with consequences that have been in turn destructive and productive.

(Titoism was born totalitarian. In so far as it remained a monopolistic political system, and never renounced economic, social and cultural claims, it always had at least totalitarian aspirations. Since it became, as already remarked, autocratic rather than totalitarian, it acquired a specificity that it owed to the circumstances of history. Its very isolation had forced it to open out. Direct, brutal and massive repression gave way to indirect, relatively sophisticated and selective restraints. Mass media took over from the secret police and other security services as the permanent welding force.

The People's Liberation War was not only the historic source of the Titoist regime, it was also its constant inspiration. The revolutionary struggle, waged by the partisans recruited, trained and led by the Communist Party of Yugoslavia, is presented as both a revolutionary and a patriotic enterprise, with the emphasis changing according to circumstances. Cleverly kept up, the confusion between the two allowed effortless and endless changes of register, enabling Tito to be called, not entirely without contradiction, head of the resistance, liberator, leader of the revolution, and father of the fatherland.

Keeping up the memory of the civil war did, however, mean rejecting half the population of the 1940s and placing them in the camp of reaction and collaboration. Officially, then, their war dead remain in hell. It has

48

generally been claimed that Yugoslavia was one of the 'most resisting' nations, the People's Liberation Army growing to 800,000 by the end of the war, and suffering 305,000 dead. But more recently it has also been said by Yugoslav military historians that she was one of the 'most collaborating' nations, contributing 350,000 armed 'quislings'. All this is not conducive to healing war wounds and rallying patriotic feelings in a country where historical memories have a very long life.

If the authorities had managed till recently to drill into the young the official interpretation of the partisan war, it was by ceaselessly playing the same tune – clarion call degenerated to muzak – from nursery school upwards, and by boring them with tales of legendary times. Decades would elapse before other truths began to appear in Yugoslavia in the historiography of the Second World War. Meanwhile, by dint of epic, the human element of that period has almost been destroyed. Having become cynical and materialistic, younger Yugoslavs may never understand what preceding generations went through.

Born Stalinist, Titoism became non-aligned and self-managed. Its non-alignment, however, was never the mere refusal to align with this or that super-power. The Belgrade government actually persisted in wanting to lead a progressive movement of non-aligned states.

Tito generally encouraged Eurocommunism, which he saw as a potential Communist club without constraints, one which his own Communist Party could have advised, perhaps even led, and one which, in return, could have backed his own resistance to Soviet pressure in international Communist gatherings. In the end, non-alignment seemed to linger on only because Tito was there to preside over it. Yugoslavia, by that time, was alone again, even though no longer under any immediate threat.

British and American political scientists agree that self-management has become, for better or for worse, part of the political culture of the Yugoslavs. In the absence of political pluralism, it has – so we are told – introduced economic pluralism. In theory, it appeals to some other regimes that are attracted to socialism yet repelled by the repressive nature of Communism. Finally, in the absence of the sort of indigenous private capital capable of taking over large enterprises, Yugoslavia could not, even if she wanted to, get rid of her self-management, unless she were to return to old-fashioned state interventionism.

A brilliant idea in terms of ideology and publicity, introduced as far back as 1950, self-management was fifteen years taking off. Since then it has continually changed, tossed about by new Party programmes, legislative reforms and theoretical statements. The situation has always been such that any critic who wants to correct this or that aspect of it can always be accused, by those who do not share his approach, of being against the very principle of self-management. Yugoslav officials, economists, even simple managers, have long been stressing its drawbacks and failures rather than its advantages and successes.

A good manager in Yugoslavia must know the intentions of the Party, the relatively simple laws of the market, and the infinitely more complex ones of the legislatures. He must satisfy both the political authorities and the self-management organs, without forgetting the consumers. Party, legislation, works council and consumer do not always agree, and usually disagree in periods of crisis. In other words, to be a successful manager one must be able to unravel within one's own mind the inconsistencies of a system which, theoretically and officially, has abolished contradictions.

Economically, the best time for self-management would have been the 1950s, in an industrial context of small and medium-sized concerns – except that it had not yet got moving at that time. The system in its present form could arguably be a useful model for an economy of industrial take-off, but it is also arguably no longer suited to an economy that has become highly industrialised and market-oriented. Politically, however, self-management has been exploited as an all-purpose slogan intended to show the inherent originality of the Yugoslav system. A useful myth to be opposed to that of central planning, it helped to move away from the Titoist imitation of Stalinism to what would become mature Titoism. Failed experiment, panacea, illusion, self-management needed the framework of an authoritarian state to survive. It has eventually been turned into a substitute for political democracy, and now serves the needs of neither political democracy nor economic efficiency.

The discords of Titoism were harmonised to a large extent by Tito himself, the conductor of the Yugoslav orchestra who was life-president of the Republic and of its ruling party, supreme commander of the armed forces, fellow of all the academies, doctor of all the sciences, holder of all the honours. Over what used to be the usual representation, rose-coloured and emotionally charged, of an original and advanced Communist society dominated by its benign yet charismatic leader, can be superimposed another, that of an autocratic system, pulled apart by its contradictions but held together by a ruler who, despite appearances, was a revolutionary turned conservative.

The cult of his personality equalled that of the most prominent dictators of the twentieth century. Enzo Bettiza, Dalmatian-born Italian journalist and senator, in a discerning book on European Communism (*Il comunismo europeo – una verifica critica dell'ipotesi eurocomunista*, Milan, 1978) distinguishes between two types of political eroticism – the 'forum'-type (*da piazza*) eroticism of Nazism, a display of mass-projected homosexuality, and the 'chamber'-type (*da camera*) eroticism of Communism, an expression of sublimated, almost religious love. On that scale, Tito's cult would fit half-way between Bettiza's two types.

Another synchroniser of internal differences within the Yugoslav system was propaganda, and propaganda was one of Titoism's most successful achievements. Mediterranean boastful loquacity with esoteric verbiage works wonders in the West, as Mussolini discovered long before Tito. A year after Tito's death, the then US secretary of state, Alexander Haig, wrote in the visitors' book of the late president's mausoleum in Belgrade: 'A great leader and a world statesman who had led the peoples of Yugoslavia out of the ruins of war, to stability and prosperity at home, to respect and prestige in the world' (as reported in the Belgrade daily *Politika*, 4 May 1982). But only a month or so before Mussolini's declaration of war, the then British prime minister, Neville Chamberlain, was still expressing to the Italian ambassador his admiration for *il Duce*, 'the greatest man in Europe' (as recorded by Giuseppe Bottai, one of Italy's Fascist 'hierarchs', in his diary, after seeing Giuseppe Bastianini on his return from London: *Diario 1935-1944*, Milan, 1982). The quotations are translated back into English.

Verbal inflation had increased between 1940 and 1981 to the same degree as the world has shrunk, but one forgets nowadays the credit enjoyed by Italian Fascism at its beginnings, a credit that came not only from the right. People saw in it an interesting social experiment. Even more important, Fascist totalitarianism was so much more moderate, so much more open – in short, so much less totalitarian than Nazi totalitarianism that the Western powers tried for a long time to use Mussolini's Italy as a counterpoise to Hitler's Germany, which was so much more frightening. The press, when it does not over-dramatise, has a tendency to facile optimism. It often wants to believe in the words that substitute for acts, in order to find what it is looking for. In the case of Yugoslavia, it is what distinguishes her system from that of the Soviet Union.

The constraints of geography and mentality

Anyone who watched Tito's funeral on a television screen on 8 May 1980 and has also seen newsreels, photographs and reports of King Alexander's funeral on 18 October 1934 must have been struck by similarities. The same streets of Belgrade were lined with people who not only had the same features, but who also expressed their grief in the same way. The style of the pageantry had changed; the mentality appeared to have survived almost unaltered.

The respective reigns of Tito and Alexander both now belong to the past, and the historian cannot but be struck by the elements of continuity. These are obscured by the all-too-glaring revolutionary upheavals, by the specifics of Titoism, and by our thirst for headline changes. The Communist revolution and the Turkish conquest some five centuries earlier are the two solutions of continuity of Balkan history, yet neither was absolute. Cultures survive radical change. Having seen how Titoism became an original system, it is worth looking for ways in which it fits into a tradition.

Left on its own, it adapted to a situation that naturally reflected the constraints of geography and mentality. The demarcation lines that went through the Balkans, and the Yugoslav lands in particular, created 'grey zones' rather than 'iron curtains'. The non-aligned posture was but the latest in a series of historical situations where Yugoslav territories found themselves to be neutrals or intermediaries. Going back to the medieval Serbian monarchy and the city-republic of Ragusa (Dubrovnik), such situations provided the conditions in which new ideas were born, economic development was launched, political independence was maintained, decline was cushioned, or dependence was made acceptable.

When they emerged into the modern world in the nineteenth century, the political élites of these lands quickly found out how to insert themselves into inter-power relations. Since they could not muster enough strength to contribute to the formation of an international order, they tried at least not to link themselves exclusively to one of the great powers. As far back as the risings against Turkish rule at the beginning of that century, the Serbian leaders Karageorge and Miloš Obrenović (the founders of the two dynasties that were to alternate on the throne) turned to France and Britain for some sort of insurance against total dependence on the Austro-Russian alternative. Much was made of this in the summer of 1987, when '150 years of diplomatic relations with Serbia/Yugoslavia' were commemorated to offset a hardened British attitude to Yugoslavia's debt problem. At a later stage, Serbia having obtained home rule, her chief minister Garašanin came to realise, towards the middle of the nineteenth century, that only a unified South Slav state, turned towards the West, could be truly independent, and prevent an Austro-Russian takeover.

In the twentieth century, between the two world wars, Yugoslavia, along with other smaller nations of Central-Eastern Europe, displayed her best diplomatic ability to developing an international order – that based on the Versailles settlement and the League of Nations – which she saw as being favourable to her own interests. In times when such favourable factors emerge, Yugoslav foreign policy generally tends to play an important role in trying to consolidate them.

One can detect a tradition of trying to balance, or of juggling with, the influence of the three geopolitical forces of the West, the Germanic power, and Russia. This translates an ambivalence of feelings towards the three which, in psychological terms, can be scaled down to an opposition between Europe and Russia. On the one hand, Yugoslavs feel a nostalgia for, and an attraction towards, Europe as they realise that Russia is a dominating power with little to offer by way of civilisation. On the other hand, an emotion of Slav solidarity usually outlived the disenchantment with the Russian connection, for it was reinforced by disappointment with European expectations and, in the case of Communists since 1948, by the belief that the Soviet system remained fundamentally socialist in spite of everything.

Titoist foreign policy would probably not have cared to acknowledge this ancestry. Even less would it have seen any link with the policy of its immediate predecessors. As minister of foreign affairs in the government-in-exile during the Second World War, Ninčić, a veteran of inter-war European diplomacy, thought of a post-war continent placed between the two poles of Britain and Russia. Reacting against the idea of a bipolar world, he wanted his country to be part of a wider bridge between the opposed interests of these two powers, not the instrument of one or the other of them. Earlier in the war, while Prince Paul was trying not to get involved, two strands were detectable in his neutralism – a tactical one towards the Axis dictatorships, and a strategic one towards the Western democracies.

The latter states are interested in only one aspect of whatever 'Yugoslav way' the Belgrade government is trying to tread – its independence and apparent stability. The West is anxious that Yugoslavia should not cave in to the pressure of the threatening power of the day – German

Reich or Soviet Union. It fears that centrifugal forces might be released as soon as the Yugoslav helm is no longer firmly held. It supports all successive strong helmsmen, provided that the discipline they impose is not such as to raise qualms in its collective liberal conscience. Thereby a Western diplomatic attitude is perpetuated which puts up with accessories of Yugoslavia's regimes, those of the strong helmsmen – King Alexander or Marshal Tito – and those of their not-so-strong successors who do their best to ensure the continued existence of the authoritarian regime they have inherited.

The survival of mentalities is the other channel through which continuity flows. Great changes have been accompanied by migrations, which bring back to the surface mentalities of an earlier age. The Turkish conquest, the Habsburg imperial reconquest and the wars of liberation have all been followed by an exodus from the conquered/liberated regions, then by a settlement as the new rulers brought in soldier-settlers. The newly-conquered or newly-liberated lands, usually under-populated, were more often than not ready to receive excess population from the highlands, where older ways of life had been favoured. Every successive wave of such 'invasions' by the men from the mountains had served to refresh historical memories.

The seizure of power by the Communist Party, just like the Ottoman conquest, did away with the visible forms of the old order, and for a while, cut off the territory from the rest of Europe, thus allowing more archaic mentalities to surface again. Furthermore, in the post-revolutionary period of the 1950s and '60s, the new intelligentsia that was being mustered contained a good number of elements from the former educated élite who had managed to adapt to the new order.

Obviously no single homogeneous political tradition emerges from the constraints of mentality and geography, but there are different traditional elements that meet and bolster one another. The political unity of Yugoslavia is not merely due – as is often superficially stated – to the interests of the powers that wished it into being, and to the magic of the divinely-inspired great men who performed the miracle of unification. Yugoslavia was indeed born prematurely, but if delivery was hastened by the First World War, her conception resulted from the common elements that already existed in the culture and in the way of life of its components. To this similarity of civilisation one must now add the bonds woven by seven decades of shared experiences. These are the ties that somehow hold Yugoslavia together, rather than her charismatic lawgivers with their ruling parties, armies and bureaucracies.

Alongside organic growth and power apparatus, external threats should also be taken into account as factors of unity, for as long as they do not turn into aggression. At that point, and when the aggressor sets about brutally exploiting internal differences, the bonds give way, as happened with the German attack of 1941 and with the Ottoman advance at the turn of the fourteenth century.

Nationalism did not arrive in these parts directly from France and North America, but by way of Germany and Italy, with all that romanticism had added to it by way of pseudo-spiritual attributes and irrational energies. With no well-defined territorial framework, nationalism swerved backwards and forwards between realistic populism and idealistic mysticism. These oscillations have only served to reinforce the diversity of historical experiences. Federalism would have been the obvious way to coordinate the differences, had it not been so alien to the political traditions of the South Slavs. Ritual invocations were made to it between the two world wars, but with little understanding of the workings of that particular form of government. When the Communists adopted it, they gave it no political content. It developed in time as a cultural, an administrative, even an economic federalism, but it was only with the eventual federalisation of the Party itself that it made its way into the political tradition of Yugoslavia, unhappily squeezed between Tito's 'kingship' and the 'federalisation' of the Party hierarchy.

The diversity of historical experiences can be reduced to the two major traditions which met in 1918 and have confronted each other ever since – Serbia's political tradition, unitary and centralist, looking to the French model, and Croatia's, born of the ethnic and constitutional complexity of Austria-Hungary. For the Serbs, their Orthodox Church – the only surviving institution of the medieval monarchy – had continued the development of a conscious historical entity during the centuries of Turkish rule. In the nineteenth century, the growing embryo of a Serbian state provided the framework within which nationalism and politics could blossom, and contemplate the liberation and integration of kindred populations. This tradition assimilated emancipation from Austrian and Hungarian sovereignty to the wars of liberation against the Turks. From such a point of view, the Yugoslav state was but the final stage in a long process of liberation and unification.

The historical experience of the Croats was that of the continued separate existence of the 'Crown of Croatia'. It fell to the nobility, the only survivor of their medieval monarchy, to continue the task of giving shape to a conscious entity during the centuries when that crown belonged to foreign dynasties. The struggle for its rights had managed to keep its constitutional existence as a form in which nationalism and politics were able to develop under the Habsburgs. Invaluable though they were, Croatia's institutions were worth more for their form than for their content. National and political action in Croatia continued to be the prerogative of a limited élite, the bourgeoisie taking over from the nobility. In 1868, in a Hungaro-Croatian sub-compromise to the Austro-Hungarian compromise of 1867, it obtained some measure of home rule, and for half a century thereafter that élite brought to near-perfection the act of political bargaining. By 1918 it yearned for a Yugoslavia where an enlarged and reinforced Serbia would have been balanced by an extended and consolidated Croatia.

If the Serbian perspective was focussed on centralism, the new Yugoslav state was perceived from the Croatian point of view as an improved dualist system which would have strengthened Croatia's autonomous status. During the initial years, the constitutional debate was less of a confrontation between centralism and federalism than a contest between unitarism and dualism. The outcome was influenced by three additional factors that lent their support to the unitarist tradition. There was the Yugoslav idealism of part of Croatian opinion, added to the fear felt by many that a small and isolated Croatia would not be able to stand up to strong outside pressures. There were the Serbs of the former Austro-Hungarian empire. More than all the other Yugoslav subjects of the Habsburgs, they had looked to Serbia as the Piedmont of the South Slavs. Her political structure had proved its worth, and it was they who insisted on rigid centralism. Finally, there were the regional aspirations of the smaller groups, combined with the existence of secondary traditions, which turned to the central government for privileges or protection.

At the time of the risings against the Turks, on the territory that was to become modern Serbia, society was more communal than patriarchal. Whereas authority rested with the group, it was delegated to headmen whose authority was conceived only as the emancipation of their respective groups. Serbia having acquired her autonomy along with a greater consciousness of herself, the despotic authority of her prince-liberator, Miloš Obrenović, was no longer perceived as being that delegated by the collectivity. From the time when new men began to rise from the peasantry, and new ideas and new manners to filter in to the principality, Prince Miloš's paternalistic rule was no longer accepted. The peasants too felt the need for a guarantee of the 'rights' they had acquired in the course of a revolution that had removed the military, political, social and economic bases of foreign rule.

That revolution ended up by turning into a struggle for power between the new oligarchy and the prince. The notables were opposed to the institutionalisation of the ruler's authority. They wanted a return to the group's delegated authority. The persistence of this attitude to authority is to be found all through the history of modern Serbia and later also in Yugoslavia. It can help us to understand the circumstances in which authoritarian governments are accepted or rejected. In Serbia, opposition has always been more political than nationalist, hence a tradition of liberalism in the intelligentsia, and even of radicalism in its student avant-garde.

Opposition in Croatia has, on the contrary, tended to be nationalistic rather than political. Since the middle of the nineteenth century, the political class there has generally lived in an atmosphere of intellectual dissent rather than around a real power-structure. Real power was far away, for the political élite no less than for the peasantry. However, whereas part of the élite was pushed in the direction of power by the fear of external threats, the peasants were less and less willing to be ruled by, and to fight for, a king in a distant capital.

The swings within the Croatian national movement between populism and idealism could turn into confrontation between the two tendencies. The populist tendency is a moderate one. It endeavours to defend or to promote the interests of the population of Croatia's territory, in agreement both with forward-looking political forces in Serbia and with the government in Belgrade. The idealist tendency is extremist. Its aim is to restore Croatia's historic individuality whatever the obstacles and the cost. Every time it is cut off from its populist roots, the Croatian national movement becomes concerned more with abstract aspirations (the rights of the Croatian nation) than with concrete aims (political democracy or social progress).

A blend of traditions

What has the blend of these traditions produced? First and foremost, an ambivalent attitude towards authority, an ambiguous response to authoritarian regimes foreign or native, a double legacy of expedient submission and of bragging rebelliousness. Defiance and accommodation alternate and even co-exist. It is generally assumed that those in authority have got to where they are in the pursuit of personal advantages. Relations between citizens and office-holders consist, as far as possible, in the exchange of personal services. The individual Yugoslav loves freedom, which means essentially his own freedom, but he also cares for an ordered society, and may even not be adverse to a benevolent despot, to impose some discipline on others. There have always been groups ready to come to an arrangement with the rulers so as to obtain special advantages. There is no lack of time-servers who alter their labels in order to follow the political fashion of the day – usually that of government, but also that of opposition.

The Croatian political élite seeks simultaneously the help of the Serbian opposition and some sort of compromise with the authoritarian government. At a time when they are afraid of their own nationalist extremists, and when the government is ready to bargain so as to divide the opposition, Croatia's political leaders lean towards the government in Belgrade. When Serbian political forces are ready to come to terms with their Croatian opposite numbers, and when Croatia's idealistic tendency raises its voice, the government is prone to use the apprehension of those Serbs outside Serbia who are frightened of finding themselves under the rule of Croatian nationalists. Scared by the threat of Croatian separatism to a united Yugoslavia that gives them the supreme advantage of living all under one roof, Serbs tend to rally round the government which sets itself up as the defender of the common polity.

The opposition has never yet been more than a coalition of different interests brought together by their disparate disagreements with those in power. Pursuing both short- and long-term aims, most of these groups are ready to turn their backs on the opposition alliance if they can obtain concessions from the government. The aims are more 'national' in the Croatian tradition, and more 'political' in the Serbian tradition, but the mentality that underlies both has become the same. Between 1927 and 1971, variations of this political game have been played through the different phases of the monarchical regime and of the Communist regime.

Yugoslavs have never been true monarchists, in the doctrinaire and legitimistic sense of the word, but they have often given the impression of being in need of a 'king' – a leader with whom they can identify their collectivity. Not all their 'kings' have been crowned heads, or even heads of state, or even heads of government. There was King Alexander, and there was Marshal Tito – the latter more of a 'king' than all the kings that preceded him. But one also thinks of Pašić, Radić, and even General Mihailović. They were architects of liberation, unification, or

revolution, or simply symbolised aspirations. One is proud of the auto-
crat who pushes one's country into the limelight, who is received on an
equal footing by the great leaders of the world. One loves the 'king' for
as long as one can identify with him, especially when one is linked to the
cause that he represents. And when such a 'king' dies, it can be sensed
from popular grief, orchestrated yet genuine, that he had become a
symbol of Yugoslavia's unity and independence.

To such sentiments, the rulers respond with a series of postures that in
turn contribute to shaping another political tradition. Governments
attribute magic powers to constitutional acts, legislative statutes, plans,
proclamations, messages and letters issued by the ruler, to flags and
slogans, but also to interdicts, in order to iron out difficulties and differences. The pre-war monarchy lost patience with the Serbo-Croatian
question that it had inherited from Austria-Hungary. It then tried to
impose a negative solution by prohibiting the expression of sectional
nationalism, and by fostering a feeling of official Yugoslav patriotism.
The Serbo-Croatian question was thus removed from the agenda of open
political debates. As for the Communist regime, it adopted the principle
of ethnic multiplicity on the Soviet model. Yet it prevented any
expression of nationalism that strayed beyond the specific limits assigned
to it, and it fostered a feeling of Yugoslav socialist patriotism. Open
dialogue and political debate were still not on the agenda.

For King Alexander, the political parties threatened to destroy the
undertaking for which he and so many others had fought. Tito felt the
same about the different tendencies within the Communist Party. Forty
years apart, the one and the other intervened to 'safeguard Yugoslavia',
and tried to impose unity of one kind (ethnic) or another (ideological).
The one, like the other, appeared as the mainspring of the country and
system. The one, like the other, eventually had a constitution tailored to
his needs yet also designed to ensure the survival of his achievement.

Tito's Yugoslavia also recalled certain aspects of the Austro-
Hungarian tradition. Catholic-inspired, the old monarchy was, in
theory and in origin, a personal union of different historic lands. It bound
together its diverse populations by a common loyalty to the dynasty, and
by the cult of a sovereign who reigned by divine right, with the sanction
of history, and with the help of a ruling class which had come to stand
above its ethnic origins in order to safeguard its social position and its
political order. In Tito's Yugoslavia, the Party, or rather its leadership,
inspired by Marxism-Leninism, ruled what was, in theory, the union
through revolution of different national groups, by virtue of an

ideological right sanctioned by history. The leadership linked the populations by a common loyalty to the Party, and by the cult of the marshal-president, through a ruling class that can be defined in terms similar to that of Austria-Hungary.

In both cases, there is an apparatus of individuals of different regional and ethnic origins, driven by the same solidarity of power and privilege, sustained by the same loyalty to the venerated person of the ruler. Like the imperial and royal authorities, so too the leaders of the League of Communists have learnt how to divide and balance nationalities as well as tendencies within the ruling class. One of the prime concerns of the government is that the components of the state should find no other bond of unity than their loyalty to the order hallowed by history.

A comparison could finally be made with the Ottoman Empire, where the established religion of Islam (other religions being merely tolerated) was identified with a ruling caste that exercised its authority over nations ('*millets*') of different forms of expression and worship, in the name of the Sultan-Caliph. By reigning so long, Tito had eventually inserted himself into all the political traditions that had followed one another in the Yugoslav lands, combining characteristics inherited from all the preceding regimes, from Austria-Hungary and the Ottoman Empire, through the various authoritarian stages of the Obrenović and Karadjordjević dynasties. At the end of his reign he had become, like Prince Miloš, a man of the past and a dead weight. In both cases, the regime was eager to remind its subjects and citizens that what had been achieved by the revolution and since the revolution had been so achieved because of the prince, and could either be repealed by him or go with him. The people, however, had come to want to turn these achievements from privileges into rights. The country needed to be freed from its liberator.

Fighters and intellectuals

Old rulers are myths, and myths are important in the political traditions of the South Slavs, who love to stress their historical claims to fame. They are good at transforming their defeats beyond all recognition by dwelling on the heroism that accompanied them – from the battle of Kosovo in 1389, when the massacre of Serbia's feudal nobility by the victorious Turks impressed contemporaries as a portentous event, to the 'eight offensives' of the People's Liberation War that were also eight successful anti-insurgent drives by the Germans. Those who had to knuckle under knew how to embellish their defeat in order to make up for the humiliation, and restore morale. The legends of an idealised past have provided strength and cohesion by instilling into people the necessary faith in a better future. By showing them that, in the past, their successes had been equal to those of the 'great' nations, the South Slavs' claims to fame have also provided compensation for their present underdevelopment.

The tendency to settle into the military epic that preceded the establishment of the political order is a dangerous one in more ways than one. Not all share this inspiration. Royal Yugoslavia used to perpetuate the memory of the wars fought by Serbia from 1912 to 1918, whereas a large part of the population, and the Croats in particular, had inevitably fought on the other side during the Great War. Communist Yugoslavia perpetuates the cult of the partisan war of 1941–5, whereas this was first and foremost a fratricidal war between Yugoslavs. From a military point of view, looking back to the victorious strategy of the last great war as a lesson for the future is a mistake that has cost many regimes dear, including that of pre-war Yugoslavia.

Yugoslavia has always been paid the compliment of being thought militarily stronger than she is. The Yugoslav governments themselves have derived benefit from keeping up an illusion of strength. The military history of the Yugoslav populations, enriched with folklore, has provided us with yet another myth: that the South Slavs' valour in fighting against their enemies has made them wellnigh invincible. The Yugoslav tradition of the nation in arms and of the general uprising springs from two sources. One has to go back, on the one hand, to the resettlement by the Habsburgs, in the seventeenth century, of South Slav immigrants from Ottoman territories in a frontier area – the Military Border – to bolster up the defence of the Austrian Monarchy against the Turks. Thereafter, Croatia of all the provinces provided the greatest proportion of soldiers to the Emperor's armies. On the other hand, one must go back to the Serbian risings against Ottoman rule and to the wars of independence.

The Defence Law of 1969 has based Yugoslavia's new strategy on the concept of the nation in arms. That law, which set up a General People's Defence, in fact has a direct ancestor in Prince Michael's People's Army Law of 1861. The great innovation of the reign of Michael Obrenović of Serbia was the introduction of a militia. It was economical, and it fitted in with the idea, perpetuated since the insurrections, that it was enough to give the peasant a rifle and minimum instruction. In the 1860s Serbia's militia made a tremendous impression, and it helped Prince Michael in his foreign policy. But, put to the test in the war of 1876 against Turkey, the strategy of the general uprising failed, and it was only the technical innovations of the late 1890s that laid the basis for the successes of the small Serbian army in the two Balkan wars and in the First World War. At that time, the nation was truly united under a representative government, fighting popular causes. Around its army, Serbia was then, as it had never been before, and has never been since, a nation in arms. In these wars, irregulars were also used, volunteers operating behind enemy lines, in conjunction with the regular army.

The inter-war Yugoslav army remained much on the same basis, with its old Serbian structure, even if it became less homogeneous by absorbing Austro-Hungarian elements that were integrated not altogether without mistrust. Though many of them hardly proved loyal in the collapse of 1941, the Yugoslav army had faithfully stood by the monarchy through its vicissitudes, and no ethnic stress was felt in the officer corps until the Second World War. The army was widely believed to be stronger than in reality it was. It did consider plans for guerilla warfare based on previous experience, but the country was led till the eleventh hour by a government that could hardly claim to represent a majority of public opinion, and the German onslaught brought about an almost instant collapse.

The ethnic imbalance of military cadres is an ongoing problem in Yugoslavia. It is due to the fact that the state was unified in 1918, and reunified in 1945, following a world war in which, speaking very generally, Serbs fought on the side of the winners, whereas Croats – or at least what appeared as a formal political entity with the name of Croatia – were on the losing side. Existing cadres of the Serbian army provided the basis for the officer corps of the new royal Yugoslav army. Few superior officers of the Austro-Hungarian forces could or would be transferred. Time was needed (in practice the whole inter-war period) before new generations of Croatian officers, trained in Yugoslav military schools, would reach the top of the hierarchy.

Similarly, the cadres of the new Yugoslav People's Army were initially provided by the officers of the partisans' army, which contained a majority of Serbs, because resistance had long been primarily a Serbian phenomenon. History thus repeated itself. Another Yugoslav military tradition is to impose blinkers on officers. Before the war, they were denied the right to take any part in politics. As a rule, they should not even have read the newspapers. Most of them thus had no political understanding. Today, they belong to the Party, are fully indoctrinated, and do not have the right to travel abroad, except in the course of duty.

Ever since Yugoslavia has existed, it has been the victim of ideologues who wanted to force human and historic realities into their conceptual moulds – of Yugoslav ideology and Communist ideology – instead of working through and with these realities. Unity has always been imposed through dogma, slogans, rhetoric and texts, because it so happened that the demiurges of unity had the backing of a majority, or of force, or of history. 'Socialism' is being talked about endlessly today, very much as 'Yugoslavism' used to be in the 1930s, without anyone really knowing what it means.

Since the 1960s, the ruling élite has broken society up into its component parts – professional, economic, territorial and ethnic – and reorganised them into hierarchies. To ease their task, the leaders have drawn heavily on the techniques of worship and of advertising. They have also made good use of diversions, real or apparent.

The individual has been held on a leash – one that has become longer and longer, so that he has usually forgotten about it when going about his everyday business, but felt it as soon as he has wanted to move further away. The master has also pulled it from time to time, to remind the individual that he was effectively held on a leash. Linked to the system, how do the intelligentsia react? The non-conformists are in a minority, just as before the war. The majority, for long kept quiet by concessions and flatteries, cared essentially for their professional privileges, cultural as well as economic. They could be called the service intelligentsia, most of them time-servers of shallow principles. When the regime is seen to lose its prestige, some of them are prone to somersaults, always in search of flattery, and devoid of political consciousness.

That is one tradition, but it is counteracted by another – that of the intelligentsia as the vanguard of political progress. The partisans of strong government have discouraged it, to say the least, and many intellectuals have often betrayed it. Nevertheless, in several instances before 1914, the exertions of intellectuals have helped the Yugoslav peoples to come out of various blind alleys into which they had been pushed by extravagant ethnocentrism or by political sclerosis. Such intellectuals wanted to know the historic, as opposed to the mythical, past. They also turned to Europe, the Europe of civilisation, as opposed to a Europe embodied in this or that 'order'. Some intellectuals in Yugoslavia today are looking for that way again.

5

THE NATIONALITIES AND THE STATE

The triune Karadjordjević realm

Yugoslavia is special in that it is neither a homogeneous nation-state (not even a so-called one) nor a truly multinational country (in spite of the guide books), but the political union of several South Slav, or Yugoslav, ethnic groups. Serbs, Croats and Slovenes originally came together to form what was at first called the Kingdom of the Serbs, Croats and Slovenes. The Bulgars also belong to the South Slav family, but the relationship is primarily linguistic, and the Bulgars went their own political way in the nineteenth century.

We have seen in earlier chapters that the similarities and interests of the Yugoslavs have been strong enough to give birth to a Yugoslav movement, to overcome the obstacles that had moulded them into several distinct historic entities and lead them to a common solution of their existential problems, and to keep them together in spite of the crises they have gone through. To these Slav groups must also be added true ethnic minorities, of different and non-Slav origin. No single one of the groups in Yugoslavia has an absolute majority. Every one of them forms a majority of the population in a given territory, and is a minority else-where. However, it is not always easy to know where their respective 'fatherlands' are, because populations and territorial names have tended to move over the centuries.

Serbs and Croats make up the core of the Yugoslav population. They are intermingled, they speak the same language (Serbo-Croatian or Croato-Serbian officially, but in fact usually called Serbian or Croatian), they have the most ancient collective self-awareness, and they feel different. Together they form an absolute majority – somewhere around 64 per cent of the population in 1921, 56 per cent in 1981.* The classic

---

* These figures and all the others that follow are more or less rounded off. They come from the first Yugoslav census (1921) and the latest to date (1981). The statistics of the former regime, as opposed to that of the Communist regime, contain no mention of 'nationality'. The figures for 1921 have been obtained by bringing together spoken language and religious faith. The percentage of Serbs in that census has been worked out from the number of Orthodox Serbo-Croation speakers, adjusted to take into account Serbs of other faiths and non-Serb Ortho-

distinction by religion – Serbs being Eastern Orthodox and Croats
Roman Catholic – does not account for a certain number of Catholic
Serbs, or even of some Orthodox who considered themselves, or were
considered, to be Croats, but especially it does not consider the two
million or so Slav-speaking Muslims. Nevertheless, it does remain the
symbol of the differences – as will be seen in Chapter 7 – although the
only valid definition nowadays is the one taken from what is stated in
the 'nationality' rubric of censuses.

The Serbs are the most numerous nation (around 40 per cent in 1921,
36 per cent in 1981), followed by the Croats (24 per cent in 1921, 20 per
cent in 1981). On the eve of the collapse of the Habsburg empire, these
two groups and their Slovenian cousins to the north (8.5 per cent in
1921, 7.8 per cent in 1981) had already fully developed such attributes as
a modern language, a literature, a national ideology, political parties, and
a strong aspiration after greater unity. How far the peasant masses shared
such feelings is a moot point. Their views did not go far in societies
where the intellectuals voiced both their own aspirations and what were
assumed to be those of their respective national communities. One could
say that these communities had both been attracted to one another and
kept apart by the forces of history.

Unification was the work of long-term factors, and the consequence
of immediate causes. The Yugoslav ideology was the child of intellectuals, but more generally it had developed among the élites. It had moved
in circles, concentric and intersecting, and it had progressed irregularly.
When Austria-Hungary broke apart, the union of its Yugoslav territories with Serbia – an organised and recognised state with a high international reputation – was the only way out of a chaotic situation.

In Croatia, the people who had helped to bring about the creation of
the new state came from the traditional parties, which represented the
bourgeoisie and the intelligentsia, because of the restrictive franchise in
the Hungarian part of Austria-Hungary. The main actors had been

---

dox – essentially Macedonians, who were not recognised as such at the time. Ivo
Banac estimates the percentage of Serbs at 30 per cent (*The National Question in
Yugoslavia*, Ithaca, N.Y., and London, 1984), Bogoljub Kočović at 41 per cent. I
am grateful to Dr Kočović for allowing me to see his computations for 1921, which
he has not included in his book on the victims of the Second World War in
Yugoslavia (see chapter 9, note, p. 131). The percentage of Serbs in 1981 corres-
ponds more simply to the number of registered Serbs. It does not include 579,000
Montenegrins, a distinct category since the war, and does not take account of
1,219,000 registered 'Yugoslavs'.

The Improbable Survivor

believers in the intrinsic unity of the South Slavs. They had ended up by accepting the centralising tendency that was being thrust upon them by the economic and social chaos, foreign threats to their homeland, and the actual existence of Serbia. The HSS (Croatian Peasant Party) only came into its own when the Croatian peasantry received the franchise in Yugoslavia. Its electorate had had enough of fighting for a sovereign and a government that ruled over Croatia from a distant capital. Its leaders distrusted the Serbian state. They wanted to preserve their land's specific identity because they had a social programme which they wanted to carry out in Croatia. They had formed the unfathomable concept of a peasant democracy, and had no experience of a parliamentary system.

The Constitution of 1921 expressed the strength of the Serbian tradition, and it managed to hold its own for seven-and-a-half years because the other, smaller ethnic groups did not present the same problems as the Croats, either because the united state seemed to them a necessary safeguard of their interests, or because they had not yet fully developed a distinct collective consciousness.

After Albania, now officially rid of religion, Yugoslavia has the highest concentration of Muslims in Europe – 1.3 million in 1921. Apart from the Albanian minority and the remaining Turks, Yugoslav Muslims are Serbo-Croatian-speaking Slavs living in Bosnia and Herzegovina (6 per cent of the total population in 1921, 8.9 per cent in 1981). Their religion – that of the ruling caste in the Ottoman Empire – had made them immune to the nationalism that had turned their Christian compatriots into Serbs and Croats. Their political reawakening took place when the Congress of Berlin in 1878 transferred them to Austria-Hungary. Their leaders wanted to preserve their own class privileges while rallying the Muslim peasants to ensure the survival of their community as an ethnic group. After 1918, they would generally preserve their identity as 'unspecified' Yugoslavs of Muslim faith.

Pre-war Yugoslavia had two political parties with an ethnic-religious base – the Yugoslav Muslim Organization and the Slovenian People's Party, the latter standing for the rural world of Slovenia. The Slovenes were one of the three recognised component groups and they also enjoyed the added advantage of living as a compact population, with a distinct language, in a well-defined area. Catholic and clerical, politically conservative and socially-minded, the Slovenian People's Party was able to become the party of local administration in Slovenia. The support of these two parties was sought by government coalitions and opposition blocs alike, so that they changed sides to defend their respective particular interests. Their leaders held cabinet office intermittently between 1918 and 1931, and thereafter continuously to 1941.

Harshly ruled by the Ottomans, and the theatre of all the wars fought in the Balkans since 1876, Macedonia had lived through a period of anarchy that culminated in the Balkan Wars of 1912–13. These had been wars of liberation from Turkish rule, but also wars of expansion pursuing strategic aims. The neighbouring states quarrelled over the area with soldiers and bandits, with teachers, priests and consuls, with politicians and historians. Its inhabitants were divided, turned into super-Bulgars, super-Greeks and super-Serbs, or made to feel second-class citizens in their respective states. They voted for the left as soon as they had half a chance to do so. Yugoslavia's Macedonians disliked being submitted to Serbianisation because they were both Orthodox and Slav-speakers.

Yugoslavia also had true and proper non-Yugoslav minorities, officially recognised as such – 16.67 per cent of the population in 1921, including 513,000 Germans, 470,000 Magyars and 442,000 Albanians. The first two groups were increasingly taken in tow by the governments in Berlin and Budapest respectively. The Albanians, who lived in the most peripheral area of the vast central belt of the Balkans that was still part of the Ottoman Empire up to the Balkan Wars, were in demographic expansion in comparison to the Serbs who had been moving out of the area. Since Turkey had been defeated and rolled back to Constantinople, Serbia acquired not only the greater part of Macedonia, but also the Kosovo region with its numerous and hostile Albanians. All Yugoslavia's southern territories, so recently Turkish, were generally underdeveloped and underpopulated as a consequence of war and anarchy. The Yugoslav agrarian reform was carried out there at the expense of Moslem landowners and to the benefit of Serbian settlers, veterans of the recent wars.

Serbs and Croats

The Serbs were, on the whole, satisfied with the constitutional framework of the Yugoslav state. They saw in Yugoslavia a natural extension of their fatherland. Not only was there no explicitly Serbian political or national movement, but it can even be said that unification put an end to any further development of a Serbian collective consciousness. Divided as they were into regions and parties, far from seeing themselves as a domineering element, the Serbs rather imagined themselves to be the ultimate defenders of the unified state for which they had given up their own identity. Eventually, there did develop a tendency which considered that this had perhaps been at the expense of the Serbs' own group interests.

Whereas the ultimate aspirations of Serbian nationalism had been satisfied, the disappointed Croats immediately demanded a revision of the Constitution. As they were not numerous enough to alter the structure of the state by regular parliamentary means, they soon diversified their tactics. Crossing over from opposition to government, and from government to opposition, the political leadership of the Croatian majority negotiated with both sides to see which of them was ready to make greater concessions. It wanted to start again from the beginning, with a new constitution that would take into account the interests of the three component national groups. A fraction of Croats, however, were to turn to violence.

Parliament became a confused arena where ideologies, social claims and ethnic grievances clashed angrily. Revolving around the Croatian issue, however, the national problem remained essentially constitutional. Yugoslavia's tragedy was that the public forum of its parliament was closed down in 1929, and its removal prevented any further debate between the various conceptions of the state envisaged by political parties and ethnic groups.

The programme of intensive Yugoslav patriotism fostered by King Alexander's personal rule, far from reinforcing their sympathies for the common state, merely increased the Croats' feeling of alienation. Cut off from its parliamentary activity, the HSS changed its nature. From a party that voiced the aspirations of the Croatian peasantry to political democracy and social justice within a Yugoslav community, it turned into a movement sensitive to the new mood of Croatia's urban classes. That mood was more concerned with the rights of their nation than with political or social reform, and the pace of transformation was quickened by the indirect influence of the Ustashas. Their secret and revolutionary organisation had but few adherents in Croatia, but the dissatisfaction on which it fed spread after the king had granted the Constitution of 1931. More than ever, the Croats were united against centralism, whatever might be their political tendencies otherwise.

Even so, the immediate consequence of King Alexander's assassination was to bring all Yugoslavs together. Most Croats had at least valued his foreign policy, and an overwhelming majority of Serbs had respected the late monarch even if they had not always approved of his methods of government. Nevertheless, the Serbs too were disappointed. In order to preserve what to the Croats appeared more and more as a regime of Serbian hegemony, they had had to give up their political freedoms – the fruit of some eight decades of political struggles. With the end of a genuine parliament, their political parties – parties of political representation – lost the reason for their existence and began to disintegrate. The process by which they had started to link the inhabitants of Macedonia and the Serbs of the former Austro-Hungarian lands to the common institutions was brought to a halt. After the king's death, that feeling of disappointment grew under the regency of Prince Paul, for whom Serbian opinion did not have the same respect.

Contacts were taken up again between the Serbian and Croatian oppositions in order to devise a way to challenge the authoritarian regime, and reorganise the state according to an agreement between the political parties, so as to satisfy a majority within each of the component nations. The programme of the united opposition thus obtained the backing of a substantial majority of public opinion in the late 1930s. Most Serbs were conscious of the need to give satisfaction to the Croats, if only to remove the government's permanent argument against a return to a truly representative regime.

Eventually, however, it was with the regency that the Croatian opposition came to an arrangement. Both sides were hard-pressed by the international situation. The HSS was increasingly worried by the radicalisation of Croatian opinion. The regency was troubled by the rising tide of opposition, and wanted to divide it. A few days before the beginning of the Second World War, as a matter of urgency, the monarchy tried to improvise a solution. The setting up of a province of Croatia with a special status was accepted by the Slovenian and by the Muslim party, but it put an end to the united opposition, and caused an unfortunate upsurge of bitterness on both the Serbian and the Croatian side.

Many Croats were already of the opinion that the concessions did not go far enough. The Serbs felt humiliated and depressed: Croatia had obtained rights that were being denied to the rest of the country. Serbian opposition leaders were opposed to the adoption of half-measures, which they considered to be worse than nothing because they drove a wedge between Serbs and Croats at a time when a common front was more important than ever. There was resentment against the HSS which had dropped its opposition partners in order to join the government. When the recast cabinet ended up by giving way to German pressure, its adhesion to the Tripartite Pact was the straw that broke the camel's back as far as Serbian opinion was concerned.

The coup that toppled the regency, and brought forward King Peter's coming-of-age, installed an all-party administration and created an illusion of national unity which the German attack would soon dispel. The Yugoslav state and the Yugoslav idea which underpinned it had held as well as could be expected, in spite of tensions and crises, both domestic and international, for as long as the country had been at peace. The Axis destroyed unified Yugoslavia, but not permanently, for it was to come back to life, in another form, with the defeat of the Axis. The destruction of Hitler's Reich not only destroyed Yugoslavia's militant centrifugal nationalist forces that had jostled for little places in the 'New Order'; it also eliminated the largest of Yugoslavia's non-Slav minorities with the expulsion of half a million Germans.

The eightfold Communist republic

When the Communist Party came to power, Yugoslavia was restored as a multinational state of related nations, thus taking advantage of the monarchy's failure to weld together the separate identities of Serbs, Croats and Slovenes into a single national consciousness by means of a centralised state structure and an official ideology of 'Yugoslavism'. The new federal division added to the three original groups. The Macedonians were acknowledged as a distinct national group, and Macedonia was set up as a separate republic. The same status was granted to Montenegro, whose inhabitants were encouraged to identify with the territory's historic identity. Bosnia-Herzegovina was kept undivided. Slovenia, Croatia, Bosnia-Herzegovina, Serbia, Montenegro and Macedonia were the six constituent republics of the Communist federation of Yugoslavia. Furthermore, two autonomous regions were carved out of Serbia – Voivodina in the north and Kosovo in the south, because of their mixed ethnic composition. They had been the cradle of Serbdom, at the beginning of its medieval and of its modern development respectively, but Serbia had to be cut down to a size that was not too big in comparison with Croatia. An end had to be put to what many felt to be her dominating position, and satisfaction had to be given to the differences that existed in the regions now separated from inner Serbia.

The Communist Party had on the one hand inserted itself into the spontaneous resistance of Serbs during the war, while on the other hand, it had used the notion of Serbian hegemony to win support among the other groups, particularly the smaller ones and the minorities. It put into practice a policy which aimed at balancing out the nationalities – to a certain extent against each other. It looked to the peripheral groups to weaken the central ones, particularly the Serbs and the Croats, whom it wanted to equalise. It substituted ideological integration for ethnic integration, capping federalism with a unitarism of power and ideology. Ethnic pluralism and federal forms were meant as lightning conductors for national emotions until Communism had managed to do away with them.

Nationalism developed rapidly in Macedonia, where it answered a genuine need. Political decisions there reflected designs that were both domestic and foreign. The new rulers in Belgrade were not quite sure, at first, how far they could rely on the Macedonian nationalism that they were encouraging. To them, it was a calculated risk linked to their dreams of a Balkan federation dominated by Yugoslavia. This was even more true of the Albanian minority and the Kosovo region that were built up as a bridge for Albania to cross over into the Yugoslav federation. In the meanwhile, the Communist regime was no more popular than the old regime had been. It immediately had to face a major Albanian uprising in Kosovo.

The superiority complex of Yugoslavia's Communist rulers had not endeared them to their opposite numbers in the neighbouring countries that were on their way to becoming 'people's democracies'. The break in 1948 thus came as a good excuse to shrug off Belgrade's tutelage or meddling, and nowhere more so than in Albania. Because of tension with Tirana, the authoritarian treatment of the Kosovo Albanians continued. The Bulgarian authorities did more than put an end to Yugoslav interference in their portion of Macedonia. They reversed the process by beaming propaganda from Sofia towards Yugoslav Macedonia. This incited the Yugoslav government to a new campaign of 'Macedonification' (essentially of language and history), which won over many more people to the idea of a Macedonian nation within the Yugoslav federation.

The decentralisation of the 1950s which followed the break with the Soviet bloc gave added responsibilities to regional leaderships. In circumstances where the economy was becoming partly controlled by a decentralised political apparatus, and partially directed towards regional markets, local authorities took on a greater importance, especially in the more developed republics that were also less dependent on the centre in terms of subsidies. The richer wanted to increase their self-sufficiency by retaining a greater share of their revenues; the poorer wanted to attain the same result, but by increasing their economic infrastructures in spite of their meagre means, with more federal aid. These rivalries called on local feelings, which thus found new channels in which to flow. The national problem, which had been repressed till then, reappeared, combining old emotions with new economic grievances. Regional identities clashed on the subject of the allocation of federal investment funds.

All had grievances against the federal government. The loosening of the constraints of power was generally slower at the centre than on the periphery, but it was also proportional to the level of economic development. Croats blamed Serbs for all that was wrong, and vice versa. Serbia, whose economic level was more or less on the Yugoslav average, had no particular economic ground of complaint. Her dissatisfaction was psychological: all that expressed the pride of the Serbian nation had been clipped back in order to satisfy the others. The local apparatus, too close to the centre on which it modelled itself, did not provide any real leadership. Serbian nationalism fed on nostalgia.

Croatia obviously had her nationalism as well. It was grounded on distance from central government, but it had been discredited by the war. Yet there was strong economic resentment in that republic – the feeling of being a rich territory exploited for the benefit of the less developed regions to the east and south, and of the centre in Belgrade. Grievances of that kind were even stronger in Slovenia, a yet more developed area, even more distant from Belgrade, and different too because of its ethnic, linguistic and religious homogeneity.

Macedonia and Montenegro had been consciously built up by the regime, to prevent them from listening to siren songs from Sofia or Moscow. These republics had obtained great economic benefits, and were gluttonous for federal aid. Even so, whereas Macedonia's national consciousness was becoming undeniable, Montenegro's remained very debatable, existing more in theoretical books and articles than in people's hearts and minds. It went against the trend of centuries, which had been to feel that Montenegro was a part of the Serbian nation. At the same time, a considerable effort had been devoted to winning over the Albanian and Hungarian minorities in their respective autonomous regions of Kosovo and Voivodina. Finally, the census of 1961 had officially acknowledged the existence of a distinct ethnic entity in the Slav-speaking Muslims. For want of a better name, they were called – ironically in a Marxist-Leninist regime – the 'Muslim nation'. Just as the Macedonian nation before it, it met a requirement. It gave a name to a community that had hitherto defined itself more negatively than positively.

The new constitution of 1963, by introducing at last a real measure of decentralisation, encouraged a closer association between nationality and territory. Was Yugoslavia still a federation of nations, or was it already on the way to becoming a confederation of territories? Whatever the answer, towards the middle of the 1960s the national question had come to occupy second place in the leadership's scale of worries – a short way behind the economic reforms. The mentality of the generations aged from forty to sixty was still largely pre-Marxist. Not being able to satisfy them with more political freedom, the regime turned a blind eye to their indulging in nationalism. The tactic was a dangerous one, for these emotions were passed on to the following generations, whose intellectuals, whose Communists even, began to display their national colours without the guilty conscience of their seniors.

Poisoned by the war, then frustrated without ever being exposed to any rational analysis, such mental states were often reduced to simple emotions. In so far as these were directed against the centralist conservative wing of the League of Communists, the decentralising reformists had allowed them to develop. They were particularly significant in the two richest republics, Slovenia and Croatia.

Homogeneity gave special potency to Slovenia's isolationism. In Croatia the situation was more complex. Distrustful as they were of Belgrade, the Party leaders in Zagreb did not yet dare to run the risk of being accused of Serb-baiting, or of reviving anti-Croatian feelings elsewhere in Yugoslavia. Croatia's particularism thus confined itself initially, in public at least, to discussions about language and literature. In Serbia there was a mood of irritation, even within the Party, at the way unconsidered generalisations about the 'conservative Serbs' had gone unnoticed by the leadership in their concern to move on with economic reforms. Besides renewed encouragement to an assertion of Montenegro's identity, it was in Macedonia that one could find the most intense and most blatant 'ethnogenesis' (the jargon word for 'nation-building'). It was meant to give satisfaction both to popular feeling in Yugoslavia's southernmost republic and to the political leadership in Skopje. Its necessity can be understood in the light of the fact that no more than 71 per cent of the population of Macedonia had registered as being Macedonian by nationality in the 1961 census (the figure was only 67 per cent twenty years later, in the 1981 census), with a percentage of Albanians (13 per cent in 1961, 19.76 in 1981) even higher than in Serbia (8.7 and 13.15 per cent in 1961 and 1981 respectively, for the whole republic).

Resurgence of passions

Whereas the Hungarians (504,000 in 1961, down to 427,000 in 1981 as a result of a low birth-rate) appeared to be as happy as their South Slav compatriots in the Socialist Federal Republic of Yugoslavia, the Albanian minority presented the regime with an extremely serious problem. Visible signs of resentment in Kosovo surfaced only in 1966, with the fall of Ranković, Tito's right-hand man and security chief. The relaxation of the police state then coincided with the general upsurge of nationalism throughout Yugoslavia. With the reform movement under way, and with more concessions to the Albanian minority, repression became intolerable.

Police excesses in Kosovo (where the police was dominated by Serbs) were used in the Party apparatus at large as an argument against the conservatives. The Albanian cadres of the Kosovo government machinery used them more particularly to promote the cause of their community, and to acquire popular support. An important impetus had thereby been given to Albanian nationalism in Yugoslavia, backed by a demographic thrust which had turned Kosovo into a province with an Albanian majority (77 per cent of the population in 1981). There was also an important overspill beyond the borders of Kosovo, in Macedonia, inner Serbia and Montenegro.

In 1968 there was a popular outbreak of anger in the province, with street demonstrations and public calls for a separate republic of Kosovo, even for union with Albania. Disorders spread to Macedonia. Order having been restored, the Constitution was amended in order to give autonomous provinces almost all the prerogatives of republics. Everything was done to boost the economic and cultural development of Kosovo, but dissension increased there between Albanians and Serbs. The latter, now victims of a reverse discrimination, started moving out. The former too were not particularly happy, for if standards of living had increased in Kosovo, the region still remained the poorest in Yugoslavia.

Feelings exploded again in Kosovo in 1981. With rapid social changes and a demographic surge on a background of economic crisis, the upheaval was only to be expected. The authorities, both central and local, nevertheless appeared to be taken by surprise. Once again, order was restored, at least superficially, by a show of force, a purge and symbolic gestures. However, it was not possible to raise Kosovo to the status of a republic, for a number of reasons. The main one was the ethnic balance in the federation which, since the Constitution of 1974, had become almost a confederation. The leadership in Skopje could not afford to give in to its own Albanian minority, and Belgrade could not force the Macedonian government even if it wanted to. The Macedonian cadres realised more and more clearly that a united Yugoslavia was indispensable to the future of their nation. They were in duty bound to keep up the dream of unity of the whole Macedonian nation within a greater Yugoslavia, and the federal leadership had to take account of it.

No sooner had social and economic developments led to a pluralist reaction against ideological and political uniformity than the government was faced with the same multiform nationalism it had hoped to eliminate. Meanwhile it had been able to prevent any attempt to promote Yugoslav integration by other means than those of official ideology. Nationalism does not necessarily dissolve itself in socialism. Impelled by disappointment in the present, concern for the future and nostalgia for the past, such feelings had flowed out again into old moulds. More and more nationalities had been recognised, assisted in inverse proportion to their numerical importance and to their historical seniority, so as to divide the population into smaller categories, and thus speed up their integration. Having rejected the ideology of integral Yugoslavism, the Communist regime had maintained the various ethnic communities only too conscious of their differences. It had done so sometimes in full awareness, and at other times unaware of what it was doing.

The lack of any means of free political expression for Serbian or Croatian particularism contributed once again to exciting them both. Without the possibility of discussing openly all the important problems the country had to face, national identity, because of its highly emotional character, was a question that tended to pervade all the others. The craving for more freedom of expression was all too often reduced to a need to call oneself by the name of one's nationality. From the 1960s, it turned out that the national question was much more serious than it had been in the 1930s. Then it had been a political and constitutional question only. Now it was seen to be an economic, social and cultural question as well.

After 1974, the trend towards identifying republics with ethnic groups increased the malaise of the Serbs, who had further been hurt by developments in the province of Kosovo. In the 1960s the Serbs had begun to ponder seriously on the consequences of their dispersal. Of all the nationalities, they had the highest proportion living outside their own republic. In 1981, there were a little under 2 million Serbs in the other republics, and some 1.3 million in Serbia's autonomous provinces, against 4.9 million in what is now called 'inner Serbia'. The territorial division of Yugoslavia was acceptable to them as an administrative structure; it was not acceptable as a framework for mini-nation-states. The regional apparatus in Serbia had not been able to tap local emotions. It had adhered too closely to the central leadership. As Serbian opinion felt that it had got nothing out of its government's solidarity with the federal League leadership, culture and religion picked up what the political class had not dared to handle. Serbian nationalism thus began to assemble an opposition to the regime, as Croatian nationalism had done in the 1930s.

Simultaneously, the defenders of Croatia's identity were increasingly recruited from the cadres of the League of Communists of Croatia, bringing the government of that republic to fly in the face of the central authorities. There was a feeling that the ban on the expression of Croatia's national distinctiveness had at long last been lifted. As a consequence, the government in Belgrade was once again openly identified with Serbian influence. When the central authority put an end to this heresy in 1971, and disciplined the politicians, the Catholic Church and the intelligentsia saw there was a new role they could take on.

In the more outlying regions, the more level-headed nationalism of Slovenia and the still young nationalism of Macedonia went on with the task of turning their territories into national republics. Whereas Slovenian particularism however had come to ask itself whether a looser Yugoslav community would not give greater scope to the economic development of their northernmost republic on the borders of the Western world, Macedonian particularism felt, and still feels, that it needs a strong South Slav collectivity in order to survive in the heart of the Balkans.

Shaken by the common ideological crisis of all Communist societies, the Party bureaucracy in Yugoslavia since the death of Tito clings to its power-bases in the republics as tenaciously as it is able, in order to stand up to the general malaise that is both political and social. Its fragmented nationalism, in search of a new freshness with which to restore its tarnished image, has been able so far to break up the enormous potential of opposition. At the same time, it threatens the state with the virus of disintegration, and its component nationalities with the loss of feeling for their common interests, not to mention their common destiny.

Serbs and Croats live together, sharing a language and a mentality. The territory that they inhabit cannot be separated by an amicable divorce settlement in a situation of international peace. If the Yugoslav federation were to fall apart, Slovenia would become the cul-de-sac of northern Italy and Austria, while Macedonia would be exposed to Bulgarian influences. The partition of Yugoslavia, if it could be carried out, would place her successors in a situation of mutual enmity with one another, as well as at the mercy of their more powerful neighbours. Her nationality question does, nevertheless, offer a permanent temptation to the mischief-makers of uncompromising solutions, and to all those who fish in troubled waters.

6

THE ALBANIANS – YUGOSLAVIA'S MOST
EXPLOSIVE PROBLEM

The historical roots

It was in 1981 that the world at large became fully aware of Yugoslavia's Albanian problem. Student demonstrations at Priština University in March quickly gave rise to widespread and violent riots all over the Socialist Autonomous Province of Kosovo, with serious clashes between ethnic Albanians and security forces. Unrest spread into Macedonia and Montenegro. Kosovo was sealed off, a state of emergency was declared, there was a show of force, educational establishments were closed. By November the situation appeared to have returned to normal, even though demonstrations continued to occur into the early months of 1982. The number of casualties was given as nine dead (including one policeman) and 257 injured (including 130 members of the security forces), but the wildest rumours had circulated concerning the extent of the riots and of the repression.

This had been the latest in a long series of outbreaks in the mixed Albanian-Slav territory generally known as Kosovo (Kosovë in Albanian), the roots of which go back to the Slav settlement of the Balkans. As has been the case with most migrations, invasions, conquests and settlements, this one by-passed or never reached remoter areas where previous populations remained unassimilated.* The mountainous area of modern Albania was one such region, and its history has been one of consecutive conquests never pushed through to completion, and of precarious domination by a succession of powers.

---

*   The parallel has been drawn with the Celts of the British Isles: L.Stavrianos, *The Balkans since 1453* (New York, 1958). Other useful works covering the historical background down to the First World War include: D. Djordjević and S.Fischer-Galati, *The Balkan Revolutionary Tradition* (New York, 1981); S. Skendi, *The Albanian National Awakening, 1878–1912* (Princeton, 1967); and A.Rossos, *Russia and the Balkans – Inter-Balkan Rivalries and Russian Foreign Policy, 1908–1914* (Toronto, 1981). S. Pollo and A.Puto, *The History of Albania from its Origins to the Present Day* (London, 1981); R. Marmullaku, *Albania and the Albanians* (London, 1975); and A. Logoreci, *The Albanians – Europe's Forgotten Survivors* (London, 1977), are recent 'Albanian' surveys – written respectively in Albania, Yugoslavia and the West – covering mainly the modern period.

In the twelfth century, the medieval Serbian monarchy grew in the depressions of Metohija and Kosovo, north-west of the Albanian mountains, at a time when the mountaineers first started coming down because of demographic pressure. The region now generally known as Kosovo covers the tectonic depressions (*polja*) of Metohija (literally 'the land of the priories', adjacent to the Albanian frontier) and Kosovo (shortened from Kosovo Polje, 'the plain of the blackbirds'), further to the north-west. At its peak, the Serbian monarchy dominated the feudatories of most of present-day Albania, but after the battle of Kosovo Plain in 1389 – traditionally seen as a landmark in Serbian history – came the Ottoman conquest of the region. What remained of the Serbian monarchy moved northwards, and Ottoman Turkish rule started a process of removal of the Christian lords from the best lands, as well as a general economic regression of this once rich area. Albania proper became one of those remote mountainous tracts of the Ottoman Empire left largely to their own subsistance resources.

The trend whereby the pastoral Albanians came down from the mountains to the depressions and the valleys was accelerated as they became converted to Islam. It is not easy, however, to distinguish between Slavs and Albanians among Christians before the turn of the seventeenth and eighteenth centuries. Serbian medieval sources point to the presence of Albanians in Kosovo, and there is evidence of Albanians fighting alongside Serbs in the battle of Kosovo against the Turks, and later in the Austro-Turkish wars. With the Habsburg campaigns penetrating deep into the Balkans, many Serbs, particularly the upper layers of society in the southern regions, were compromised and had to emigrate, not a few Albanians going off with them. Those who remained in what the expatriates called 'old Serbia' suffered from wars and plagues, and the population of Kosovo declined sharply. There was room for resettlement, and the Ottoman authorities favoured the expansion of the mountaineers into the peripheral areas. Whereas Albanian Christians who emigrated with the Slavs became Slavicised, many of the Slavs who stayed behind were Islamised and even Albanianised.

Starting in the 1830s, risings of various kinds periodically disturbed the Albanian-inhabited areas, and particularly the northern parts whose leaders were engrossed in local interests. They fought both for and against the Sultan's troops, reacting against the nationalist movements of their Christian neighbours, and also against the centralising reforms of Constantinople. Old Serbia and northern Albania figured in the expansionist schemes of the nineteenth-century Serbian and

Montenegrin rulers. There were strong geopolitical reasons for wanting an outlet to the Adriatic, and to 'free' Kosovo would restore the territorial link between the modern principalities and their medieval progenitor. Not only were there Serbs to be redeemed from Turkish rule, but Catholic Albanian clansmen and even other potentates of northern Albania looked to Serbia at times, though such influence did not cut much ice among the Muslims generally.

The League of Prizren, at the time of the Congress of Berlin, represented a turning-point on the road to the emergence of an Albanian movement. The great landlords and tribal chiefs came together to prevent territories inhabited by Albanians from going to the Christian Balkan states. Encouraged by the Ottoman Porte, the league provided an umbrella for many committees, leaders and interests, and its most radical supporters came from Kosovo. When the Porte eventually had to give in to the decisions of the Powers, it came up against Albanian resistance. Born of their resentment, the Albanian movement would thereafter receive assistance from various foreign factors. While Serbia and Montenegro encouraged it so as to sap Ottoman power in the areas to which they aspired, Austro-Hungarian and Italian influences were also increasingly felt on the south-eastern coast of the Adriatic.

The period from the 1880s to the Balkan wars was one of growing anarchy in the peripheral zones of the territory inhabited by the Albanians. Revolts against the central government, and Albanian vendetta guerilla action against Slavs or Greeks – with or without Turkish help – were accompanied by increased population movement. As Albanians continued to expand into the better lands of Kosovo and Macedonia, Slavs continued to immigrate into the Kingdom of Serbia from the southern regions. The Young Turks' policy of Ottomanisation and Islamisation after 1908 disappointed expectations on all sides, and turned the Albanians against the new regime. The year 1912 saw the generalised revolt of the various Albanian clans and groups. They appealed for support to the Christian populations of European Turkey as well as to Serbia and Montenegro, at the same time as they negotiated with Constantinople. With the fall of Skopje to the rebels, the Porte gave in and promised to hand over virtual control of the four provinces in which the Albanians lived (Scutari/Shkodër, Yanina, Monastir/Bitola and Üsküb/Skopje), thus appeasing the rebellion as Turkey was about to face the onslaught of its former Christian vassals.

The Balkan states went to war to vindicate the cause of their oppressed co-nationals still under Turkish rule, but they were also attracted by the prospect of expansion in Macedonia and in Albania. The Serbian and Greek governments, by their policy towards Albania, went against the ethnic principles for which they waged war. The Albanians, who had fought with the Turks ever since their demands had been accepted, turned to independence once Turkey had been defeated. The independence of Albania was proclaimed on 28 November 1912, and supported by Austria-Hungary as a second-best solution to maintaining Turkey against the expansionism of the Balkan states.

Serbia was not allowed access to the Adriatic, but she did obtain 40,000 square km. of additional territory to the south, including Kosovo. The feelings of a substantial part of Serbia's new subjects towards her were doubtful, if not antagonistic. All the provisions of constitutional rule were not immediately extended to the new territories, while Albanian emigration to Turkey, following on the change of rule, initiated a reversal of what had hitherto been the dominant population trend. Serbian-Albanian feelings were further embittered by the attitude of Serbian and Montenegrin troops whenever they moved victorious into Albanian-inhabited territory, and by the vengeance inflicted by local tribesmen on the defeated and dejected Serbs retreating through the mountains of northern Albania in 1915.

With the constant instability that ensued in Albania, the debate over borders dragged on until after the creation of Yugoslavia. Eventually a territorial settlement was achieved in 1926. This left half-a-million ethnic Albanians on the Yugoslav side, having to use Serbo-Croatian in schools – in so far as they went to school – and in official communications. Coming straight from centuries of Turkish rule, or rather non-rule, Kosovo was the most backward region of Yugoslavia. Its agriculture used only a fraction of the arable land available, and the agrarian reform carried out in the 1920s created a fund of land that was more than sufficient locally. In order to improve agriculture, and to try to redress the ethnic balance of the population, legislation provided for colonisation, with priority to war veterans. Land-hungry Orthodox Serbian peasants from the barren mountainous regions began to pour in. Quite apart from the fact that it fostered two separate communities in Kosovo – that of the Serbian settlers, relatively modern and prosperous, and the other, illiterate, uncompetitive and dissatisfied, of the Albanians, discriminated against in the land redistribution, and many of whom had to emigrate northwards as unqualified seasonal labour.

When Yugoslavia collapsed in 1941, Kosovo, along with other Yugoslav and Greek territories containing ethnic Albanians, was annexed to the Italian-run Kingdom of Albania. Whatever the feelings of Albanians towards the Axis otherwise, those outside pre-war Albania were thankful to Italy and Germany for having brought about the realisation of a national union. Once again, numerous Serbian refugees left the areas incorporated with Albania. The various armed movements generated in defence of the Serbian population in Kosovo met with the hostility of the local Albanians. Albanian auxiliaries were used against Serbian armed bands, who returned like for like. This went for partisans as well as chetniks of one kind or another, in spite of the help given by the Yugoslav Communists to their Albanian comrades.

The Yugoslav Communist approach up till 1981

Before the war, the Communist Party of Yugoslavia had appealed to all those who felt aggrieved by the Serbian-style centralisation of the government. It had talked of the right of self-determination for all ethnic groups, and as late as January 1941 was still calling on Albanians to expel Serbian settlers and occupiers. In spite of this, Communism, once in power, did not initially alter relations between Yugoslavia and Albania over Kosovo. The Albanian Communist leaders claimed it for their country, and the Yugoslav Communist regime was no less alien to the Albanian peasants than its monarchical predecessor had been. Albanians fought both with and against the Yugoslav Communists, who took over control of Kosovo, and who adopted towards this essentially hostile ethnic minority measures that differed little from those used earlier there by Fascist authorities against the Serbs. The result was an uprising (about which nothing was said at the time, and little has been said since) which broke out in December 1944, and was not finally put down till the following summer – after Kosovo had been formally restored to Yugoslavia.

The Autonomous Region of Kosmet (short for Kosovo and Metohija) was born of the Constitution of 1946. The Albanian minority of Yugoslavia had grown to 750,000 (1948 census), but a more moderate approach to it could be envisaged as the Albanian Communist Party, safely in power, had purged itself of elements opposed to Yugoslav influence. Communist Yugoslavia was taking over the role that Fascist Italy had played. She was increasingly treating Albania as her satellite, and Stalin seemed to agree in principle that Albania ought eventually to join Yugoslavia – which was a way of solving the Kosovo problem.

For Kosovo remained a problem, especially after the expulsion of the Yugoslav Communist Party from the Cominform had given Albania the chance to break free from Tito's protection, and to indulge in psychological warfare against her northern neighbour, whose Albanians remained alienated. Time was needed for Albanian cadres to be formed in the region who could really share responsibility with Serbs, and so many of the measures taken in favour of the former never went very far because of resistance by the State Security Service. Even more than elsewhere, the 'secret police' was in evidence in Kosovo, which remained a security region in fact if not in law, because of tension with Albania after 1948. The province looked calm, and it was not till the fall of Ranković in 1966 that Yugoslavia's Albanians began to show visible signs of rancour.

The ways in which that event was used to the benefit of Kosovar Albanians have been seen in chapter 5. By giving greater satisfaction to the Albanian minority, the Yugoslav leadership also helped it to become more conscious of its strength, for by 1961 it had grown to 915,000 in total, and to over 67 per cent of the population of Kosovo. In its anxiety to blame everything on Ranković, however, the government appeared weaker than it really was. Difficulties piled up during 1968, and Kosovo exploded in November. Thousands of demonstrators called for an independent university, the removal of what they saw as the provocatively Orthodox name of Metohija, the status of a republic, even union with Albania. There were clashes with the police, reported to have injured thirty-seven (including thirteen policemen) and killed one. The situation was hushed up, no foreigners were allowed into the troubled area, the army is believed to have been sent in to restore order, and many Albanian nationalists were arrested.

Turning down the demand for republican status, Tito offered more autonomy and more aid. The constitutional amendments of 1968 granted Serbia's associated regions some of the prerogatives of the republics and the style of 'Socialist Autonomous Province'. Kosovo (the name now being officially adopted to cover the whole province) was also granted the right to fly the Albanian black-eagled red flag. To keep this backward region as satisfied as possible, and to provide for its fast-developing population, the federal government laid special emphasis on its economic and cultural development. Kosovo was given priority over the other underdeveloped areas (Montenegro, Macedonia and Bosnia-Herzegovina), and a crash programme of economic development was launched. Between 1966 and 1968, Kosovo received almost 30 per cent of all funds assigned for the underdeveloped. Between 1971 and 1975, 70 per cent of its budget and of its investments came from federal sources.

The Priština faculties, hitherto extensions of Belgrade University, were turned into an independent university, and they rapidly Albanian-ised their staff, student body and tuition. Steps were taken to promote more Albanians to positions of authority; the police and Security went Albanian; and a policy of 'positive discrimination' towards Albanians was adopted in employment generally. Relations having been nor-malised with Tirana in 1971, Kosovo was able to receive books and teachers from Albania under agreements concluded directly with the Albanian government there. Tito's strategy was to give the Albanians all the cultural rights they wanted, and all the economic aid the country could afford, in exchange for their loyalty to Yugoslavia and to Titoism. It could be speculated that it was also yet another of his ambitious gambles – that the open-door policy towards Tirana through Kosovo would be used to carry his conceptions across to Albania.

As the percentage of Albanians in Kosovo went up from 67 to 77 in the two decades between 1961 and 1981, the number of Serbs (and Montenegrins – for, whatever the differences, they do not exist in Kosovo beyond the census registrations) declined, not only relatively, but also absolutely by some 28,000. Despite absolute gains, Kosovo con-tinued to slip even further behind relatively. Development, however well intended, was neither sufficient nor sufficiently well-directed to satisfy the deeper aspirations of a rapidly increasing population whose very growth rate diluted the benefits of economic growth. Distrust con-tinued to run deep between Albanians and Slavs. In spite of being dis-criminated against, the proportion of Serbs in official and managerial positions was still felt to be too high. There were recurrent demonstra-tions across Kosovo throughout the 1970s, including outbreaks of vio-lence. Between 1968 and 1981, some 600 arrests were reported in the province, as well as some eighty indictments – of both Albanians and Serbs.

As Kosovo was edging itself into quasi-republican status through the constitutional reforms of the early 1970s, and was fast losing what remained of its Serbian character, two new factors began to emerge. The Albanian minority was not an exclusively Serbian problem, but one to be shared with Macedonia whose treatment of its own Albanians was tougher. The other factor was the economic crisis, which was becoming acute in Yugoslavia, and hitting the poorest areas hardest. The author-ities had tried to meet the unemployment problem in Kosovo through a massive expansion of education, and by chanelling a high share of the aid funds into modern, capital-intensive industries – policies which soon created more problems than they solved.

The rural private sector benefited little, and there was high emigration – mostly the uneducated and unskilled, with poor employment prospects. Then, by the middle of the decade, the net increase in returning Albanian workers put more pressure on the labour market at a time when jobs could no longer be provided for the ever-increasing output of graduates. In 1981, Priština had 51,000 students (compared with 178,000 employed and 67,000 unemployed in the public sector), and about one-third of the total population was in full-time education. With thirty students per 1,000 inhabitants, Kosovo had the highest student concentration in Yugoslavia, and probably one of the highest in the world.

The 1981 riots: causes and responses

It is easy to list the causes that led to the explosion, but difficult to rationalise the feelings behind the discontent. However backward, Kosovo would be even worse off as part of Albania. The province's Muslim peasants would not wish to give up their land or their religion; there was more than one hint of anti-Communism mixed in with their anti-Serbianism in the previous round of demonstrations in 1968; since then, the resurgence of Islam in Yugoslavia had come as an additional booster. The cadres in Kosovo must have realised all that, and yet they were promoting and/or exploiting nationalism.

One can conjecture that the radicals among them wanted an enlarged Kosovo as a full republic, perhaps with the hope of one day bringing in Albania itself within Yugoslavia. This version of a greater Albania would have enabled the leaders and the younger cadres of the Kosovo Party organisation, with their better training and broader outlook, to play the decisive role, and it would also have fitted in with Tito's old dream of a greater Yugoslavia. Whatever the guesses, the presence of an independent and proud Albanian state over the border, one that presented itself not only as the champion of national unity, but also as a system that had solved all economic and social problems, without rich or poor, inflation or unemployment, was – the obvious propaganda notwithstanding – a strong emotional attraction for the poorest, fastest-growing and least integrated ethnic group in Yugoslavia. It was pre-eminently so for the increasing number of frustrated young graduates and students, especially when the local leaders made use of particularism to resist central government attempts to establish some control over the way aid funds were used, and to reinforce their local power base – only to lose control over the situation. And it was especially so too when discontent was fuelled against both federal and provincial authorities by the obvious misuse of development funds.

It is difficult to believe that the riots of 1981 came as a rude awakening to the Yugoslav government, except to the extent that they destroyed the image of Kosovo as a bridge between Yugoslavia and Albania. It was now clear that Tito's open-door policy had failed, for through it Albania had infected Kosovo. However, the leadership, both local and central, was probably surprised by the pace of events. The authorities tried at first to play down their significance, and then blamed the dirty work of traitors – before the admission, within limits, of the scale of violence led to criticism of the entire policy towards Kosovo since 1968.

The main responses were to impose stiff sentences on the militants, and to purge the local apparatus. According to official figures released at the end of March 1982, at least 2,000 people were apprehended by the police, and over 1,600 received prison sentences – more than 400 of between one and fifteen years. The blame was placed on the inefficiency of the local leadership. Some of the top provincial officials were removed, there was a widespread purge of the Party in Kosovo, and many teachers were dismissed. The demand for a republic of Kosovo was quickly deemed to be out of the question, but it was only when the Tirana Party press came out in support of the 'legitimate demands' for the unification of all the Albanians of Yugoslavia into one republic, free of Serbia's tutelage, that the accusing finger of Belgrade turned towards Albania. The war of words then began. Belgrade denounced the Albanian government for meddling in the internal affairs of Yugoslavia, and for seeking to dismember her; Tirana denounced the Yugoslav government for the crimes perpetrated in Kosovo, and for the draconian measures imposed on the province.

The top Yugoslav Party bodies met in May. Their conclusions were that nothing needed to be changed in the system, and that the cause of the trouble lay in the nationalism that had not yet been overcome. Because of lack of vigilance, and because of liberalism, it had been exploited from abroad. Manifold Albanian émigrés were at work, supported by foreign intelligence agencies and by the leadership of Albania – all intent on subverting Yugoslavia's constitutional order. At a subsequent meeting in November, the Yugoslav Central Committee called for a comprehensive programme to overcome nationalism. In practical terms, this consisted of a number of moves. The cultural and educational exchanges that had enabled the free entry into Kosovo of teachers and printed matter from Albania were stopped. A press campaign denouncing the Stalinist and retrograde nature of the Tirana regime ended a decade of self-imposed silence on such issues. A free rein was given to public revelations of what hitherto had been an official taboo – the pressures and excesses of Albanian nationalism in Kosovo, the violence, the desecration of graves and churches, the exodus of Serbs. Finally, the Yugoslav leadership clutched frantically at old Titoist slogans, and reverted to symbols such as renaming the town of Kosovska Mitrovica 'Titova Mitrovica' (the sixth town in Yugoslavia to be called after Tito, usually with the predicate 'Tito's' – the Yugoslav version of 'Regis' in England), or deciding to build a monument to Tito in Priština.

The Kosovo policy of the Yugoslav government then became more restrained. The nationalists went underground, but they continued to disseminate their literature, using Marxist-Leninist terminology, and calling for unity. Those who had been sentenced to short terms of imprisonment gradually returned home, to a warm welcome by all, including local Party and government officials. Teenagers continued to be prosecuted and imprisoned for offensive nationalist graffiti, but those responsible for the excesses that hastened the outmigration of Serbs were not to be found. Ethnic harassment and Serbian emigration had been persistent phenomena since 1966, but the authorities had not wished to acknowledge them until 1981. The net emigration of Serbs has been estimated at 102,000 in the decade 1971–81, with a further 30,000 between 1981 and the autumn of 1987. The tables had been turned on the Serbs of Kosovo: they had now become an oppressed minority, one that had further fallen from 14.9 per cent of the population in 1981 to a little more than 10 per cent in the autumn of 1987. The local Albanian cadres were strongly suspected, even after the purge, of being less than fully committed to continuing along 'Tito's way'. In December 1985, a clandestine subversive Albanian nationalist organisation, which included a number of army officers and Security officials, was discovered.

By 1987 the situation in Kosovo was again explosive, but this time it was the Serbs who had had enough. In April, 60,000 Kosovo Serbs signed a petition denouncing the situation, demanding action and warning the authorities that they would no longer tolerate the 'genocide' being carried out against their community. When one of the organisers

of the petition was arrested, thousands gathered and scuffled with the
police. Top Party officials had to be sent from Belgrade to address and
calm down the demonstrators. The whole of Yugoslavia saw the event
on television. When the top Party bodies met in the summer to discuss
the situation in Kosovo – where they feared that local Serbs would soon
take the law into their own hands – and to devise ways of ending the
exodus, thousands came up from the southern province to Belgrade.
Although there were no disorders, these were real 'marches on Belgrade' – to demand that the local leadership be dismissed, that criminal
charges be brought, and that constitutional changes be enacted to enable
the Republic of Serbia to exert some control. When the Yugoslav
Central Committee met in July, it did so surrounded by demonstrators,
with a cordon of security forces in between. This had never happened
before. Nevertheless, the Central Committee resolution did no more
than admit that Party policy had not been carried out, and recognise with
disquiet that Kosovo had become Yugoslavia's most important
problem.

Uncertainty in Belgrade, insecurity in Tirana

The federal division was made originally on the assumption that Yugoslavia was the land of the South Slavs, and that the South Slavs of different groups, when living outside their respective centres, needed no
special provisions. However, since the 1960s nationality has, in constitutional terms, become more closely associated with territory, so much so
that by the end of the decade the leaders were on the point of saying that
their country was no longer the federation of the South Slavs, but the
state of all those who lived on the territory of socialist Yugoslavia – Serbs, Croats, Slovenes, Macedonians, Montenegrins, Muslims,
Albanians, Magyars, Turks, Slovaks, Romanians, Bulgars, Italians,
Czechs, Ruthenes, Romanies, Germans, Vlachs, Russians, Poles, Jews,
Greeks, Austrians, 'undecided', 'various' and 'unknown' (the categories of the 1961 census). Ethnic proportions could thus vary in time
without upsetting any balance. That was a convenient conception. On
the one hand, it ensured that not a square centimetre of that socialist
territory would ever be ceded, for no neighbouring nation-state could lay
claim to co-nationals who, on the Yugoslav side of the border, were
Italian- or Albanian- or Magyar-speaking citizens of the SFRY. On the
other hand, it enabled the Yugoslav government to take an interest in

the fate of those co-nationals of the majority groups who lived over the border.

Since 1981 official pronouncements are again saying that Yugoslavia is the motherland of its South Slav nations. The Albanians, whose motherland is the Socialist Republic of Albania, are merely a 'minority' (a 'nationality', as opposed to a 'nation', in official parlance) in Yugoslavia. As such, they cannot have the nations' right to self-determination, and create a 'state' within Yugoslavia that would have the theoretical right of secession. (The right of self-determination is, however, deemed by the constitutions to have been excercised once and for all during the People's Liberation War.)

In practical terms, to reconsider the original territorial division would open a Pandora's box. A republic of Kosovo would be an irresistible pole of attraction to Albanians living in Macedonia and Montenegro. Its establishment would jeopardise the loyalty of the Macedonians, whose 'state' would be squeezed between Albanian and Bulgarian territory, and between greater-Albanian and greater-Bulgarian aspirations. It would open the way for the demands of other ethnic groups seeking autonomy from republics in which they find themselves a minority – notably the 532,000 Serbs of Croatia, who are not only different from the Croats, but also different from the Serbs of Serbia at least as much as the Montenegrins. It would lead the Serbs to fear for the territorial integrity of Yugoslavia, which satisfies them, with the consequence that dissatisfaction in their midst tends to manifest itself in political rather than in nationalistic terms. It could also signal a rapprochement between Serbia, Montenegro and Macedonia, all more or less sensitive to the Albanian problem. And so on and so forth.

Anyhow, is the often heard assumption that the problem would be solved by a republican status correct? But for the status symbol, provinces now have all the rights of republics, and nationalities are equal to nations since the provisions enacted in 1968. Furthermore, the provinces of Kosovo and Voivodina can veto decisions taken at the level of the Republic of Serbia, whereas the opposite is not true. That is why the demand has been voiced by Serbs, both in Kosovo and in Belgrade, for a change in the status of the provinces so as to give the republic some real control. A diminution in the prerogatives of Kosovo would, however, also go back on an institutional set-up that now satisfies all the federated units but Serbia, since it legalises all particularisms in their relations with the centre. That set-up, adapted from the legacy of the Comintern, and moulded by Tito over the years, is the principle by which Yugoslavia claims to have solved the national problem. As yet no leader would dare challenge it openly.

What makes the Kosovo crisis more difficult to appease is that it coincides with a bleak economic climate of rising inflation, rising unemployment, and cuts which reduce growth in general, but more particularly the funds available for public spending, hence for Kosovo pain-killing. The government has run out of ideas, and is unsure of itself. It must know that it bears part of the responsibility, in so far as it has always been the policy of the Yugoslav Communist Party to balance ethnic groups against each other.

The Albanians were well entitled to believe that a Communist regime in Yugoslavia would treat them in accordance with earlier appeals for their support in the struggle against 'Serbian hegemony'. This, however, did not actually come about until the post-1968 era. Then, the official Tirana interpretation of history – that of a continuous and predestined Albanian national consciousness, going back to the Illyrians, over the whole territory inhabited by present-day Albanians – was allowed to become no less orthodox in Kosovo, in order to keep its new intelligentsia happy. The Serbs, on the other hand, know that the change of the proportion of Albanians to them in Kosovo is eventually due to the disparity in birth-rates (35 per thousand for the Albanians, 2 per thousand for the Serbs, in 1986), and additionally to the fact that, in so far as they are able to, they tend to leave the poorest part of Yugoslavia, in search of higher standards of living elsewhere. Now, however, that outmigration has turned to flight as a result of unchecked pressure, thus resuming under a Yugoslav, even a Serbian, Communist government a process that they associate with the Turkish yoke, Serbs increasingly perceive it all as evidence of their national decline under socialism.

In its Albanian context, the story of the origins of the Communist regime can be read in terms of increasing interference by its Yugoslav patrons up till 1948, when their excommunication put an end to that, and the pro-Yugoslav elements in the Albanian power structure were purged away. The leaders of Albania viewed with awe the subsequent Yugoslav-Soviet reconciliation; they feared that they would have to pay for it, and automatically allied themselves with those who seemed determined to prevent it. Albania eventually broke with the Soviet Union in 1961, settled into the obscure role of a Chinese client, and survived as a Balkan backwater of Stalinism.

With the Yugoslav-Chinese rapprochement of the late 1960s and early '70s, Albania began to show signs of wanting to come out of its isolation, and there was an improvement in relations with its neighbours. This was seen at first as following the Chinese lead, and then, with increasing evidence of stress in Sino-Albanian relations, as a hedge against the consequences of this growing rift. In 1971 Albania's relations with Yugoslavia were officially normalised. Throughout the decade, various links were established, and, after the break with China in 1978, Yugoslavia became Albania's principal trade partner. Already after the invasion of Czechoslovakia, Albania's leader, Enver Hoxha, had offered to fight 'shoulder to shoulder' with the Yugoslavs. At the time of Tito's final illness, Albania repeated its readiness to fight for Yugoslavia.

Was this all in sharp contrast with the stand adopted only a year later, when the Kosovo crisis erupted? Throughout the 1970s, in spite of improved relations, and even though it advocated an increase in trade and cultural exchanges, Hoxha's government remained uncompromising in matters of ideology. The 'normalisation' was not all that smooth. The hard ideological approach to Yugoslavia remained, as part of the Albanian regime's self-proclaimed role as custodian of true Marxism-Leninism-Stalinism. It is obvious that uncertainties over the country's future position in the world at least partly explain the rifts in the leadership, and the purge of the mid-1970s, during which Tirana actually applied the brake to the process of rapprochement with Belgrade.

It was in 1979 that Hoxha's memoirs appeared, describing the anti-Albanian activity of the Yugoslav Communists during the war, in the immediate post-war period, and after 1948. They tell of a conversation with Tito ('the King of Belgrade') in 1946, when the Yugoslav leader was alleged to have admitted that Kosovo should really belong to Albania. Hoxha nevertheless admitted that he was also told he would have to wait until the Serbs had come to understand the need for this, and Stalin later explained that it had been Tito's intention to take over the whole of Albania. This was not actually taken up in Yugoslavia until the 1981 crisis, when the Albanian press gave prominence to Hoxha's allegations, and had an easy job quoting from Tito's writings of the 1930s denouncing the oppression of Albanians in Kosovo.

Hoxha's allegations were dismissed as 'falsifications of history' at the Yugoslav Central Committee meeting of November 1981, when it was stated that, on the contrary, the Albanian leader had been the one to say at the time that his country would naturally join Yugoslavia in the near future. This coincided with the Eighth Congress of the Albanian Party, when Hoxha endorsed the moral support that had been given to the 'peaceful demands' of Kosovo to become a republic, and attacked Yugoslav, Soviet and Chinese revisionism. Since then, propaganda from

Tirana has continued, at regular intervals, to single out Serbian revisionism and chauvinism for castigation.

The war of words reveals a sense of insecurity in the Albanian Communist Party no less than in its Yugoslav counterpart. The break with China must have put Albania's decision to pursue a course of almost total political isolation to a severe test. One can imagine that the leadership, both in the last years of Hoxha's life and since his death in 1985, has been facing the question: where do we go on from here? In its history as a separate nation-state since 1912, Albania has been under the tutelage of, successively, Austria-Hungary, Yugoslavia, Italy, Germany, Yugoslavia again, the Soviet Union, and China. There have already been indications of feelers put out in several directions. Sooner or later, it will probably have to seek economic and even diplomatic support somewhere. The end of the Hoxha era could well lead to a period of domestic instability, with the champions of China, the Soviet Union, Yugoslavia and the West engaged in a power struggle.

The Kosovo issue in the early 1980s was, perhaps, already part of it. Was it meant to divert Albanian opinion from an internal crisis (marked by Shehu's suicide – not the first suicide in the leadership of Communist Albania)? Was it intended to prevent the rapprochement with Yugoslavia from going any further, or to warn Yugoslavia off? The Soviet Union has been offering Albania a resumption of relations. It is seeking friends in Tirana, but there is no real evidence of Soviet involvement in the Kosovo crisis. Hoxha also maintained to the very end that his country was ready to co-operate with all, except with the United States and the Soviet Union. He also stressed that Albania's policy, far from endangering Yugoslavia, actually defended her.

Since Yugoslav spokesmen have been saying very much the same of their own country's policy towards Albania, one should point out the limits of the verbal polemics between Belgrade and Tirana. In its open pronouncements, at any rate, the Albanian government has done no more than express support for a Kosovo republic, separated from Serbia, as a homeland for Yugoslavia's ethnic Albanians. Yugoslavia, for its part, has protested against Albanian interference and cancelled cultural exchange programmes, but there has been no question of blocking Albania's foreign trade, which has opened up essentially through Yugoslav territory. The rhetoric has not prevented the signing of trade agreements, the maintenance of an air route, or the establishment of a rail link. It is as though both sides tacitly agreed on its limits.

Not enough is known of the outlook of the agitators in Kosovo and of the support that they have been receiving. However, it can safely be said that their reactions are emotional, and that they express dissatisfaction with the situation as it is. This dissatisfaction may be Marxist in its mode of expression, but it has found in nationalism a ready-made channel into which to rush, and occasionally, though privately, it expresses anti-Communist feelings as well. It is an indictment as much of the system as of its territorial framework. The nationalism of Kosovo's new Albanian intelligentsia is first cultural, and only then political, as was that of the new Serbian intelligentsia of Austria-Hungary in the nineteenth century. It does not necessarily imply an unconditional desire for union with present-day Albania. But if Albania were to re-enter the real world, and become an attractive proposition, could Yugoslavia keep Kosovo as a semi-colonial problem, at best of the Northern Irish, at worse of the Algerian type? On the other hand, if Yugoslavia were to become a more open and pluralist polity, it could perhaps, at least until Albania followed suit, keep Kosovo by turning it into a centre of Albanian life, culture and economic development which beamed out to Albania. A view of the future, one which had imagination, could be introduced into the existing context, which would see both sides brought together in closer association, one based on mutual interest and genuine equality. For the time being, they both have at least one element in common, besides being Communist one-party states: the fact that they are independent of the Soviet Union. They could put it to good use.

7

RELIGION - THE CLAN TOTEM

Orthodoxy, Catholicism and Islam

The border between the Western and Eastern Empires ran through the lands where the Slavs came to settle, and their settlement in the Balkans coincided with the rise of two new powers whose influences would again meet over the same area – Byzantium, the heir to the Eastern Empire, and the realm of the Franks, which saw itself as successor to Rome in the West.

Springing from these two sources, whose streams overlapped for a time across the territory of present-day Yugoslavia, Christianity consolidated the fusion of scattered Slav tribes. The first royal crowns were received from the papacy, but integration was probably more rapid among the populations that had adopted the Eastern form of the Christian religion. The reasons were the Slavonic transposition of the Byzantine liturgy, and the principle followed since the Council of Nicaea of adapting the organisation of the Church to political geography. Separate monarchies developed from the tenth century – a Croatian realm soon linked to the Crown of Hungary (a link that held until 1918), and a Serbian one through the close alliance of the dynasty with the local, 'autocephalous' church. The Middle Ages came to a close with a new division between the Muslim empire of the Ottoman Turks, whose Sultan was considered to be the successor of Mohammed, and the Habsburg Monarchy whose Catholicism was the embodiment of the Counter-Reformation. These conquests brought about the most important migrations since the settlement of the Slavs, which further mixed the populations, but never blended them because of their division into political empires and religious denominations.

In Chapter 4, we saw that in Croatia it was the nobility – the 'nation' in the juridical sense of the word – that continued the genesis of a national consciousness, whereas it was the Church that carried on a similar process among the Serbs after the elimination of the feudal class. The Orthodox Church had been integrated into the Ottoman mode of government, either in the form of the single patriarchate of Constantinople for the united 'Orthodox nation', or of several ecclesiastical institutions when this was better suited to the aims of Ottoman policy.

94

At the end of the sixteenth century, the Sultan restored the Serbian patriarchate of Peć in order to have within his dominions a spiritual authority (it was also much more than that) responsible for the Orthodox Slavs, at a time when they were moving north and west ahead of the Turkish advance or in its wake. Following the stabilisation of frontiers in the seventeenth century, the Serbian patriarchate in Ottoman Peć extended its authority over believers who had become subjects of the House of Austria or of Venice, and who lived among mostly Catholic people. The Serbian hierarchy, as indeed all the Orthodox, had accepted the rule of the Sultan as being both temporal and temporary. Even though Rome was seen as a dangerous and mistrusted rival, the facts of geography and politics led the Serbian Church to turn to the Catholic sovereigns of the Habsburg dynasty. This collaboration resulted in further migrations, the exile of part of its hierarchy, the weakening of the patriarchate of Peć and, finally, its abolition in 1766.

At the juncture of Latin and Greek Christendom, the Bogumil heresy – the Balkan counterpart of that of the Albigenses – had grown in the feudal class of Bosnia, thus giving this central region its characteristic division into three faiths. At the time of the Ottoman conquest in the fifteenth century, Bosnia itself had been largely restored to Catholicism by the missionary activity of the Franciscans, while Herzegovina, along with the eastern fringe of Bosnia next to Serbia, was mainly Orthodox. The declining heresy was concentrated in northern Herzegovina. Its division had left the area without a solid ecclesiastical organisation, and its population without deep religious beliefs. This is shown by frequent changes of faith. In the century following the conquest, there were numerous conversions to Islam, from all classes and communities, attracted by the conquerors' dynamic faith. The Bosnian lords, in particular, became Muslims and thus part of the new order.

Whereas the Catholics, associated with the Sultan's enemies, were often persecuted, the Orthodox adapted themselves to Islamic rule, but in conditions for which they had not been prepared by the Byzantine inheritance. While submitting itself to the world, the Eastern Church was also overtaken by it. As the Ottoman system did not differentiate between ethnic and religious identity, the two merged, and Orthodoxy weakened as it divided into nations. With the revival of the state as embodiment of the nation in the nineteenth century, nationalism took over religion, turning the regionalism of the Orthodox Church into a cover-up for ethnic separatism. Under Russian influence, the new Balkan states reduced the Church to a form of official nationalism.

Meanwhile it had inserted itself into the Habsburg Empire as a framework for the 'Serbian nation'. After the withdrawal of the Turkish tide,
the Emperor did not restore the frontier regions to the nobility of 'Civil
Croatia'. He kept the 'Military Border' under his direct authority by
bringing in military colonists, who were largely Serbian and Orthodox,
organised into self-governing communities, and enjoying the freedom of
their own religion. The dignitaries of the Orthodox Church thus came
to be considered as the leaders of the Serbian nation in the Austrian
Empire. Settled on the border with the Ottoman Empire, the Serbs
enjoyed a particular situation, recalling that which they had known on
the other side of the frontier, and differing from the regime of the other
populations of the Monarchy. The Orthodox metropolitanate of
Sremski Karlovci (Carlowitz) in southern Hungary became, especially
after the patriarchate of Peć had been abolished, the main focus of
Serbdom, cultural as well as spiritual.

More than a religious institution, it made up for the lack of a ruling
class, and kept up the memory of medieval political forms. With no territory, and no representation in the diets, it depended, in a Catholic
empire, on the protection of the Vienna court to stand up to the pressures
of the institutions of Hungary-Croatia, in return for which it was ready
to support the reforms undertaken by the central government. Such a
relationship was a source of friction with the traditional local authorities,
which wanted to reimpose their order on the reconquered territories,
and which resented the privileges granted to the free peasant-soldiers and
to the Orthodox religion. In contrast, the Catholic Church in Croatia
identified its interests with those of the 'nation'-nobility, as indeed it did
in all the lands of the House of Austria, but more particularly in the
dominions of the Crown of Hungary. That mystical association between
'crown' and 'nation' eventually brought the privileged estates of Croatia
to yield much of their autonomy to Budapest in order better to stand up
to Vienna.

Nevertheless, Orthodoxy and Catholicism did not inspire important
political movements among the South Slavs. For the carriers of modern
nationalism in the Balkans – the secularised intelligentsia – the Orthodox Church was merely an auxiliary in a struggle that set its sights on
non-religious ends, and the Church followed their lead. For believers
who were not very keen on attendance at services, the Church was the
symbol of venerated traditions, the embodiment of a past both glorious
and painful. Priests were no spiritual advisers. They had little theology or
education. However, they did share both good and bad with their flock,

and did not lag behind them in the sphere of national and political action. Serbian Orthodoxy preached a religion of the nation, but it did so without fanaticism or intolerance. The French historian of the Serbian Church in the nineteenth century, Jean Mousset, noted in 1938 (*La Serbie et son Eglise, 1830–1904*, Paris) that the God to whom Serbs prayed was so concerned with their fate that he seemed to have been created just for them. Devoted body and soul to the dispersed Serbian Orthodox nation, the Church claimed to be its sole authorised interpreter. It propagated the belief in a kingdom that would reunite the whole Serbian family.

As the 'frontiers' of the nation were not those of the Serbian state, the Church almost inevitably came to oppose the government when the latter's 'national policy' no longer fitted with the former's conception of Serbdom. After full independence had been acquired in 1878, the Serbian government, which had never refrained from interfering in ecclesiastical matters when it deemed it necessary, tended increasingly to turn the Church into one of its departments. It was so much a thing of the nation that it was almost natural that its administration should be part of the business of government. Its bishops readily took to being civil servants, in the service of the state as well as the nation. Such conceptions occasionally aroused the dimmed hostility of the lower clergy who, as individuals, often took an active part in politics, but they also produced a divergence from the young and pro-Yugoslav section of the intelligentsia. The Church did not understand aspirations that went beyond its own denominational horizon, and as such it would long be an obstacle to a spiritual drawing-together of Serbs and Croats. Divergences there were, but never a *Kulturkampf* or anti-clericalism, for there never was any clericalism either.

In the Austro-Hungarian Monarchy, the Catholic Church was one of the pillars of established order. It supported the nobility during the *ancien régime*, before turning to the Catholic dynasty in the remodelled monarchy. In its hierarchy it was then as 'denationalised' as the higher nobility, so that nationalism in nineteenth-century Croatia, in order to assert itself, had to look either to the dynasty or to other South Slavs. In the first guise it would isolate itself in an absolute form of Croatism; in the second, it would pick up more strength by becoming Yugoslav. In the last quarter of the century, a party advocating the 'pure' right of Croatia recommended a dynastic and exclusive brand of Croatism that was hostile to the Serbian Orthodox minority in the land – a substantial one since the re-integration of 'Military Croatia'. On the other hand, it

was a Catholic prelate, Bishop Strossmayer, who was the leading personality of the Yugoslav tendency in the Croatian intelligentsia. He
believed that a true understanding of Catholic and Orthodox Christianity would lead to a better understanding between Yugoslavs.

The Catholic Slovenian People's Party came to dominate the Slovenian
countryside as the franchise was extended in the Austrian part of the
Monarchy. A combination of relative prosperity, strong religious practice and political conservatism explains the rise of this moderate, social
and clerical party that strove to obtain the most it could for the Slovenes,
who lived across several provinces ruled directly from Vienna. In Bosnia-
Herzegovina, which had been kept as a colonial condominium by Vienna
and Budapest, the Muslim Slavs had been traumatised by the end of
Ottoman rule. Convinced that their identity was threatened by nationalistic pressure from the Orthodox and Catholics no less than by the loss of
official protection, they organised themselves. Their social élite set up
the National Muslim Organization to champion the religious and cultural rights of their whole community, as well as the privileges of its
landed and trading upper crust. The Muslim Organization did obtain the
favour of the Austro-Hungarian authorities, and thereafter served them
loyally. As a political group, it strove for tactical alliances that would
enable it to maintain its dominant element. It thus came to team up with
the Croats, who were increasingly influenced by the Catholic Church of
Croatia, leaving the Serbs of Bosnia and Herzegovina as a frustrated
minority looking to Serbia.

Protected before the war, harassed after

In the unified Kingdom of Yugoslavia, there was no established
denomination, but a dozen or so religious communities were recognised
as institutions of.public law. As such they organised themselves auto-
nomously, and were granted protection and subventions by the state. *

---

*   In the 1921 census the Orthodox represented 46.7 per cent of the population (5.6
million), the Catholics 39.2 per cent (4.7 million), and the Muslims 10.8 per cent
(1.3 million). In 1931 the figures had become: Orthodox 48.1 per cent (6.8
million), Catholics 37.9 per cent (5.3 million), and Muslims 11.2 per cent (1.6
million). The other recognised denominations were the Lutherans and Calvinists
(both of them German and Hungarian), the Jews and the Old Catholics.

The first two post-war censuses also noted religion. In 1948 the Orthodox represented 49.5 per cent of the population, the Catholics 36.7 per cent and the Muslims
12.5 per cent. In 1953 the figures had become Orthodox 41.2 per cent, Catholics
31.7 per cent, Muslims 12.3 per cent.

The largest of them, the Serbian Orthodox Church, reunified under one restored patriarchate (1920), grouped all the Orthodox in the country. Unification had achieved the most ambitious aspirations of Serbian nationalism, but in a state whose ideal transcended the dream of Serbdom. An ideological gap had been established between the unitary Yugoslav state and the image of a Serbian people whose Church was its natural representative. Continuing with what it considered to be its age-old mission, the Orthodox Church oscillated politically between the government (viewing it as the guarantor of the Serbian nation in the Yugoslav state) and the opposition (when it seemed to the Church that the Crown no longer took account of Serbian interests). Thus from auxiliary to the government, it occasionally became an instrument of the Serbian opposition. This happened when the regency adhered to the Tripartite Pact in 1941, but also when the government tried to ratify the 1935 Concordat with the Holy See.

The Concordat was needed to co-ordinate the different legislations which determined the relations between the Catholic Church and the state in the different constituent parts of Yugoslavia. It was modelled on the existing concordat for the Kingdom of Serbia, and satisfied both the government and the Catholic Church. Some opposition could be expected from liberal-minded and non-clerical Croats and Slovenes, but not from Serbian Orthodox circles, and yet when the bill incorporating the new Concordat came before parliament in 1937, it was the anger of Serbian public opinion which it unexpectedly aroused.

The Orthodox Church campaigned, not against the Concordat as such, but against some of its stipulations that would have secured for its Catholic opposite number a more favourable status than its own. It was possible to argue that the Catholic Church, with its better structure and greater influence, would gain more from a unified regime of relations with the Yugoslav state. Nevertheless, and in spite of their traditional distrust of Catholicism, such an intrusion of clericalism among Serbs would have been incomprehensible but for the fact that the campaign against ratification was used essentially for political ends, to discredit the Stojadinović cabinet. The masses went along with this, because of the animosity generally felt against the prime minister's policies. Coming on top of the indifference generally shown in other provinces, the opposition stirred up in Serbia led Stojadinović to shelve the Concordat.

The Catholic Church also reacted to political realities, and came to reflect the opinion of its believers. Pillar of the Austro-Hungarian Monarchy that it had been, it rallied to Yugoslav unification, before sharing the disappointment of most Croats. However, it should be said that the disappointment of clerical Catholic circles among Croats was expressed on a personal rather than an institutional level. The majority party in Catholic Croatia, the HSS, was in any case anti-clerical. The only two religion-based parties that mattered in electoral terms – the Slovenian People's Party and the Yugoslav Muslim Organisation (successor to the National Muslim Organisation of Habsburg days) – were limited by local characteristics. In the four general elections of the 19?0s, the Slovenian People's Party obtained between 3.7 and 5.8 per cent of the votes, and the Yugoslav Muslim Organisation between 2.5 and 6.9 per cent.

Outside what could be called the constitutional spectrum, there were two marginal fascist groups. Ante Pavelić's Croatian Revolutionary Ustasha ('insurgent') Movement, born of the purist trend of Habsburg Croatian nationalism, aspired to an independent Croatia at any price and by violence. It came to symbolise an extremist Croatian opinion that was both anti-Serbian and anti-Semitic. It decked itself out with Catholic devotion because its fundamentalism needed a religious dimension to achieve radical separation from other denominational groups in Croatia – notably the Orthodox. The Ustasha movement attracted young intellectuals and students, including a number of Catholic clerics, but according to its own reckoning when it came to power during the Second World War, its pre-war adherents never numbered more than 40,000.

Not so well known was Dimitrije Ljotić's National Yugoslav Zbor ('rally') Movement. A minor political personality who had come from the Serbian Radical Party, Ljotić had been, for six months in 1931, minister of Justice in King Alexander's government. He left when his views concerning a new constitution were not adopted, and went on to found in 1935 his own movement to promote these views – a paternalistic, hierarchical and corparatist monarchy based on integral Yugoslav nationalism. After failing at the 1935 and 1938 elections (when his movement obtained 24,088 and 30,374 votes – 0.84 and 1.01 per cent – respectively), his action turned against political parties and trade unions. He eventually clashed with the government, which arrested him in 1940 and banned his movement. A devout Orthodox and an anti-Communist, Ljotić added anti-Semitism and anti-Freemasonry to his ideological arsenal. Coming more and more under German influence, his movement slid towards a variety of fascism tinged with Christian piety, and ended up as a loyal auxiliary of the German military administration in Serbia after 1941. He too attracted young intellectuals and students, including not a few Orthodox clerics, along with, in other regions, Yugoslav nationalists who wanted to put their ideal above parties.

During the Second World War, the Axis powers manipulated and incited all sectarian and ideological tensions. In their puppet-state of Croatia, which incorporated Bosnia and Herzegovina, the Ustashas accepted the Muslims as being Croats of Islamic faith, in order to turn them against the Orthodox. By showing off their Catholicism, by repeating that their policy served the interests of the Church as much as those of the nation, by using the symbolism of Croatia the outpost of the West, they got something out of individual priests and friars. Their regime, nevertheless, was fundamentally secular, leaving the Catholic clergy without much influence, and laying the Church open to criticism. The involvement of a section of the clergy in the massacres and forced conversions weakened the cohesion of the Catholic Church in Croatia.

In the central regions of Bosnia and Herzegovina where they inter-twined, the three religious communities came to grips in a ghastly tri-angular civil war. Although a relatively small number of Croats, and even fewer Muslims, had taken a direct part in the crimes committed against the Serbian population, their effect was critical in starting the infernal cycle of the fratricidal war. The very idea of Yugoslavia only came back to life with the defeat of the Axis and of its sectarian auxili-aries, and through the intervention of the Communist insurgency.

The post-war revolutionary regime adopted, naturally enough, an anti-religious strategy, but with tactical concessions to attract the minor-ities, or to show toleration for traditional practices in areas where the peasants had supported the partisans. It introduced a separation of Church and state which left the denominational communities free to attend to their religious affairs, while prohibiting the misuse of religious feelings or manifestations. These conceptions were never defined, how-ever, and their interpretation – by the political authorities – has varied in time and place.

Before the elections of 1945, the Communists, who did not yet feel sure of their power, sought an accommodation rather than a confronta-tion with the Churches, but the compromise which they sought rested on their own conditions. They pressed it by the general harrassment of clergy and the faithful. The Orthodox Church was a local Church, with no canonical links with the West. It had come out of the war with a tre-mendous prestige, acquired at a terrible price. In principle, it was ready to go on rendering unto Caesar, now a Communist Caesar, as it had rendered unto a Muslim one in times gone by. It favoured the unity of Yugoslavia, if only for the sake of the unity of the Serbian nation. The Catholic Church, on the other hand, had been weakened politically by the war and by the disastrous experience of Croatian independence under Ustasha rule, but it had strong support from abroad. It was thrown the line, which it could not take, of a position which would be more independent of Rome and nearer to 'popular feelings'.

The intention of the new regime was to limit the churches to their worship. Eventually their influence in society would dwindle to the point where they represented no more than the vestiges of a lost civilisation. The hierarchies, however, were not ready to accept separation on terms that left them without important and valued means of action. Furthermore – and although most of them had never attributed much importance to their clergy – religion played a major part in the lives of Yugoslavs and in their several national identities. So much so that in the first post-war census, in 1948, nearly everyone registered a religion, even though the Communist Party claimed to have more than a million members. After the elimination of political opposition, the Churches remained as the only institutions that did not fall under the absolute control of the Communist Party. It was thus necessary to make them harmless before they could be tolerated, and since their hierarchies did not want to understand that they had to change their ways, they would be made to understand – by obstruction, by attacks, by trials, by imprisonment.

The Orthodox Church could be tactically accepted as a patriotic institution, but it was still an implicit obstacle to the consolidation of the new order, both as a Christian community and as part and parcel of the Serbian identity. Its view of the Serbian nation differed from that held by the Communist Party. It challenged the Party's new morality, its policy of nationalities, its claim to be the exclusive interpreter of the interests of the population. A new ideological gap appeared, much wider than under the monarchy, between what Mousset called its 'old and cherished image' of the Serbian people whose Church was its authorised representative, and the ideology of a Communist state that split the Orthodox up into several groups.

The Communists' policy in Macedonia, Montenegro, Kosovo and Voivodina was contrary to the notion of a union of all the Orthodox Serbs. The Orthodox Church thus had its share of difficulties, but it was not subjected to the full rigour of the campaign that was waged against the Catholic Church.

It was the latter that had to bear the full brunt of a policy that aimed at disarming the Church. Its links with the West made it suspect. Endowed with a better organisation and with better material resources, it was deeply involved in society. Its hierarchy had stood up openly against separation, and the papacy was blatantly anti-Communist. Political movements that called themselves Catholic, however different, had left their imprints, in one way or another, in the western provinces. For all these reasons, the Catholic Church was considered to be the more dangerous. The trial of Archbishop Stepinac of Zagreb (later Cardinal) removed that danger in 1946, but at the price of turning the Catholic Church, for the first time, into a symbol of the national aspirations of the Croatian masses.

The pressures brought to bear on organised religion, on public worship and on the practising faithful were uneven, but generally on the increase until the beginning of the 1950s. Anyway, they were aimed, not at a minority, not at the reactionary remains of the past, but at the religious feelings of a large part of the population. In the 1953 census, the last one to have a rubric for 'religion', the authorities were shocked to discover that those 'without religion' amounted to no more than 12.6 per cent of the population, and that all the others continued formally to register a denomination.

It was obvious that the tough line had not been successful. At the time when, as a result of the break with the Soviet Union, Stalinism-Titoism was turning into Titoism, the anti-religious struggle became more sophisticated. In fact, the first concessions made to religious feelings could be noted as early as the end of 1950, even if they went hand-in-hand with a strengthening of the ideological front. This was intended to stop the churches from making too much of the new situation. The Law on the Legal Status of Religious Communities, enacted in 1953, gave form to the government's conception of separation, according to which it circumscribes the churches' sphere of action, confining it to their religious rites, but does not abandon its own right to intervene in religious matters. The use of violence was eventually renounced at all levels of authority, other means of pressure being always kept in reserve.

The regime had come to accept that religion would survive for several generations. It was beginning to realise that different and useful links could be set up with the outside world through the religious faiths – through the Islamic community with the Near and Middle East, and through the Orthodox Church with the Soviet Union, Romania, Bulgaria, Greece, the Anglican world, and even Ethiopia. With the election of Pope John XXIII and the convening of the Second Vatican

Council, a new attitude to Communism in the Catholic Church could be envisaged. Important changes were on their way. The death of Cardinal Stepinac in 1960 opened the way for an arrangement between Roman Catholicism and Yugoslav Communism. With the election of Patriarch German to head the Serbian Orthodox Church in 1958, and the establishment of an autonomous church for Macedonia the following year, the government could also contemplate a détente on the Orthodox side. An accommodation would take place between the political and the spiritual authorities, which was an important contribution to improving the general climate of the 1960s in Yugoslavia.

The revival of the churches

In many ways, it was the Catholic Church that had shown the Orthodox how to get out and meet the believers in a new world where so many things – balance of power, social structures, values – had changed, just as it was the Eastern bishops who had been able to show their Roman brothers how to find their place in a context that was fundamentally hostile to them. The two great Christian Churches then started to lean on one another so as to face up to common difficulties, although they rarely dared to admit it even to themselves. Towards the mid-1960s, with no collective authoritative statements, an increasing practical solidarity – on a strictly pastoral level – came to remove the religious sting from Serbo-Croatian differences.

When Cardinal Šeper left for Rome in 1968 to head the Congregation for the Doctrine of the Faith, the new spirit of everyday co-operation had already made such headway that his meeting with Patriarch German was, at the level of Yugoslavia, as important a symbol as the first meeting between Pope Paul VI and Patriarch Athenagoras. The Orthodox journal *Pravoslavlje* ('Orthodoxy') saw in the symbolical embrace of the primates a guarantee of the permanence of brotherly links between their flocks, 'who are united by one blood and one Gospel'. The Catholic *Glas Koncila* ('Voice of the Council') proclaimed: 'Never again, with God's help, will we allow other problems, however real and important, to obscure the fact of our identical faith in the Trinity.'

The Orthodox Church was then well on the way to recovery under its new patriarch. Because of its detachment from worldly affairs, Eastern Christendom had generally not opposed temporal authorities. That tradition had helped the Serbian Church to find its way in the new society, however hostile its attitude to it. It was again active in the pan-Orthodox movement, and it was also setting up closer contacts with other Christian denominations. The Catholic Church likewise, in these same years, under the guidance of its new head, Cardinal Šeper, had renovated its hierarchy, and was ready to face the reality of Titoist Yugoslavia. Inspired by the work of the Council, in which it had played an important part, the Catholic Church of Yugoslavia kept itself free of any political commitment, in order to work for a better implementation of its legal rights. The hierarchies began to co-ordinate their claims, whether in favour of the rights of teachers and soldiers to practise their religion openly, or for the clarification of the concepts of 'clericalism' and 'religious freedom', or for the real neutralisation of schools in matters of religion. The Churches began to extend their social involvement. The religious press blossomed, particularly on the Catholic side. (A survey undertaken in 1983 accounted for some 200 religious periodicals, with a total annual circulation of 15 million copies.)

Urbanisation, industrialisation, emigration and indoctrination had already destroyed much of the traditional religious context and behaviour, to the point of causing the de-Christianisation of particular regions and sectors. Nevertheless, religion continued to satisfy numerous needs, not only spiritual ones, which the Party, its organisations and its activities could not adequately meet. The religious communities also offered a way of participating in public life outside official channels. They attracted a large number of those who, dissatisfied with the order of things, sought to relate to a different world, whether the beyond or the past, to find their roots, to feel a sense of continuity or eternity in the confusion of daily life. For the young, religion had the added attraction of not being to the liking of the establishment.

The main denominations continued to draw inspiration from their traditional conceptions for their involvement in the contemporary reality of Yugoslavia. Thus the Macedonian schism in 1967, which formally confirmed separation from the Serbian patriarchate, seemed a replay of the Bulgarian schism a little less than a century earlier. Talked of as a possibility since the middle 1940s, it was strongly encouraged by the authorities. The new Church of Macedonia has not yet been recognised by the other churches of the Orthodox communion. Yet it exists, weak in its structure but supported by the authorities, notably by the government of the Socialist Republic of Macedonia, according to a Balkan tradition that sees in the Church one of the essential attributes of nationality. It owes its existence to the importance of the Macedonian factor. It is part of that strategy that uses the 'peripheral' ethnic groups to keep the 'central' national communities in their place.

The Orthodox schism in Yugoslavia marks the dividing line between two conceptions of the Church, as well as between two nations. The Macedonian Church promotes the interests of the Macedonian nation, but it does so as an auxiliary to the political authority, according to a nineteenth-century conception of the Church as hardly more than an agency of state nationalism. As for the Serbian Church, it too looks after the interests of its nation, but it does so nowadays in spite of the state, and more often than not to the distaste of the government. As we saw in Chapter 5, the decentralisation of the 1960s had not allowed Party leaders to harness local feelings in Serbia. For the Serbian masses, Serb-dom and Orthodoxy still more or less coincided. Looking for a frame-work within which they could freely express their identity, they turned to the Church. With Serbian nationalism now frowned upon, and Serbs dispersed in at least six of the eight federated units, the Church was the only Serbian institution that extended to Serbs living outside the Repub-lic of Serbia. To the extent that the state once again could not, or did not want to, fill the role of protector of the Serbs, the Church came forward to do so in its stead.

At the same time, the Serbian Church turned against the very idea of politics, intent on gathering on a different level all those who made themselves known as Serbs, and leaving politics to the ruling apparatus. It was picking up the threads of an eighteenth-century tradition. It is now impossible to imagine it renouncing the unity of the Serbian nation for the sake of the unity of the Orthodox Church in Yugoslavia. The ideological gap grows between its 'old and cherished image' of the Serbian people and the socialist state. The regime claims to have re-absorbed in its Marxism-Leninism all the problems of nationality. It takes on the monopoly of their representation; it equalises them; it allegedly harmonises them, and transcends them in a class ideology that is fundamentally anti-religious in so far as it resorts to other opiums. Juggling as it does with nationalism, it cannot allow other forces such as churches to want to represent them.

The Orthodox Church offered a refuge from the worries of the world, as well as a structure for the spiritual and cultural unity of the nation. The Catholic Church, for its part, was confident in its involvement in society; it was endowed with a relatively well educated clergy, and it was reinforced by international links. As soon as it realised that the way was clear, it sought to establish, protect and extend its 'rights', to express its point of view on morals, education and its role in society. In that way it also helped the other denominations, and contributed its strong voice to the clamour demanding a greater freedom of expression. In the Slovenian countryside, and even in the intelligentsia of the northern republic, the Church rapidly recovered an influence, although no longer a truly political one. Catholic and Marxist intellectuals struck up a dialogue in Ljubljana. Where the local Party leadership had set itself up as the champion of regional interests, it was at first more difficult for the Catholic Church to take on this role, but then, in Croatia too, there were people who felt like expressing their nationalism otherwise than through the institutional framework of the regime, and within the constraints imposed by the Central Committee.

In an atmosphere where popular conceptions identified Church with nation, where religious denominations vied with one another in organising mass religious manifestations – consecrations, pilgrimages, eucharistic congresses – and where each one of them was ever more preoccupied with its own problems, ecumenism ground to a halt from the end of the 1960s. Anyway, building bridges over the abyss created by the war between Orthodox and Catholics had been a difficult and often thankless task. The pioneers had quickly recognised each other on both sides, striding ahead particularly in the central regions where the faiths were mixed. However, the hierarchies had generally been reluctant to follow them on a path which they saw as being the right one, but which did not attract the mass of believers. Not only did the movement draw to a close, but every church actually divided up into ethnic compartments. The Orthodox Church was already split by the Macedonian schism. For all practical purposes, the Catholic Church also came to have two organisations, one for the Croats and another for the Slovenes, with the Holy See accepting this compartmentalisation to the extent of appointing an ethnic Albanian bishop for the Albanian Catholics of Yugoslavia. (Mother Teresa of Calcutta is an ethnic Albanian from Macedonia.)

However, most of Yugoslavia's Albanians are Muslims, along with the ethnic Turks and the Slav Muslims of Bosnia and Herzegovina – a little over one million of whom actually registered as such at the 1961 census when the authorities recognised them as a new ethnic category. Islam in Yugoslavia generally belongs to the Hanafi school of the Sunni obedience – the most widespread and most liberal interpretation of the Mohammedan tradition. The Islamic Religious Community (to give it its original official designation) shortened its name in 1969 to 'Islamic Community'. This was done in order to get rid of what it considered to be a superfluous adjective, but also, according to some, to identify itself better with the new Muslim 'nation'.

It had had its share of the anti-religious policy of the immediate post-war era, and that had caused a wave of anti-Communist feelings among the Islamic religious authorities. Forced to stand down in 1947, they no longer ventured an opinion on any political aspect of the national question until the 1960s. Since then, they have asserted themselves through educational and social activities in the wake of the Muslim revival, and by the building of mosques. (Of all the places of worship built in Yugoslavia between the end of the war and 1983, some 700 have been Muslim, 500 Catholic, and 300 Orthodox. If that seems to be in inverse ratio to the numbers of believers, it is because Libyan help has boosted the building zeal of Islam, whereas Orthodox churches, which always follow the traditional Byzantine style, are expensive.) Their adherents in Bosnia and Herzegovina identified themselves with a Muslim Slavism, and those in Kosovo with an Albanian nationalism that opposed Muslim Albanians to Orthodox Serbs.

A delicate balance

The process whereby religion merges with nationalism is brought to a head, paradoxically, under a regime whose ideology is both inter-nationalist and anti-religious. It is brought to a head, no less para-doxically, in a society that has already, to a large extent, been secularised. Such paradoxes are in part explained by the obvious religiosity of words and gestures of a power-structure that remains pseudo-Christian in its ritual manifestations although its ideology is anti-Christian. At a time when for so many people the clan morality of nationalism has become the only alternative to the class morality of Marxism-Leninism, religion runs the risk of becoming tribal, like everything else in Yugoslavia. Among Serbs, the protection of their historic identity seems to have been taken over by the Church, with its ancient aspiration to gather in one body all the Orthodox Serbs. Among Croats, the defenders of that identity were to be found in the Party cadres, until the central leadership intervened to put an end to that heresy. It was then, after 1971, that the Catholic Church saw its chance to acquire a new function, as it had already done in the years following the liberation and the Communist takeover. The Western Church in Yugoslavia had caught the nationalist bug of its Eastern sister.

However, the two churches have not lapsed into sectarian national-ism. They want to represent their respective nations, thus implying a national ideal that is more exalted than the autarkic one of the small federated republics. They provide nationalists with the dream image of a nation emancipated and unified – emancipated spiritually and even poli-tically. At the same time, they see to it that religion should not again be added to ethnic and regional antagonisms. Their attitude expresses a deli-cate balance, hard to express and to put across. It has been marked by another important 'summit' meeting, in May 1985, between Patriarch German and the chairman of the Catholic Bishops' Conference, Arch-bishop Kuharić, on the occasion of the second centenary of the Serbian Orthodox Church of St Nicholas at Karlovac in Croatia. The two Church leaders exchanged significant speeches about the need for their denominations to overcome the lack of trust, preach solidarity, and establish understanding, respect and love so as to triumph over the divi-sions created by history. The meeting caused much apprehension in Communist circles, which could not help feeling that since both Croats and Serbs lacked a genuine political leadership, it was more than a mere religious occasion.

The religious communities have learnt to hold back the aggressive nationalism of their respective flocks. They have also contributed a great deal to the slackening of ideological controls, by joining their own appeals to the general turmoil of the intellectual world that demands more freedom – of conscience and religious practice, of intellectual expression and artistic creation. On a more popular level, a phenomenon like the appearance of the Virgin Mary at the village of Medjugorje in Herzegovina since the summer of 1981 has been the expression, not of Croatian nationalism, but of the mood of uncertainty prevailing in Yugoslavia in the 1980s, and the general crisis of confidence in the sys-tem, accompanied by a re-examination of the past and a deep concern for the future. In spite of all that, the Serbian Orthodox and Roman Catho-lic Churches, for all their courage and wisdom in dealing with the authorities, do not yet seem able to muster the courage and wisdom which would consist in leading their believers, rather than at worst following them or at best discreetly advising them. To that extent they still play into the hands of a regime that remains basically hostile to them.

The end of 1971 marked the end of a chapter in the history of Com-munist Yugoslavia in more ways than one. Since then, relations between the regime and the religious denominations have been given a new turn.

The authorities resorted to several means to thwart the increasing role of religion. They have exploited differences between sections of the clergy and the bishops, and even provoked such differences. In all republics except Macedonia, they have renewed their verbal attacks on the churches. Since Tito's death, Party organisations have accused the religious communities of taking advantage of the crisis in order to complain about an alleged lack of freedom. A new ploy has been to appeal to the faithful.

A campaign to expose the nationalism and clericalism lurking under the cover of faith was unfurled in the course of 1985. On the Catholic side, such sins were seen to be synchronised with a worldwide resurgence of the clerical right. On the Orthodox side, they were denounced as intensified manifestations of 'pan-Serbian' nationalism. A distinction was clearly made between religious institutions and believers, since the authorities were claiming to be conducting their campaign alongside loyal Yugoslav believers against the misuse of religion by some of the clergy. The anti-religious struggle was adapted to the spirit of the 1980s, by appealing to the patriotism and socialism of the religious-minded citizens against the dishonest behaviour of 'clero-nationalist' churchmen.

The summer of 1985 was particularly intense: ministers denounced in parliament the subversive activities, rampant in all three major denominations, through misuse of the religious press, of religious instruction and, generally, of their legal rights. The patriarch and the Synod of the Serbian Orthodox Church were summoned by the government of Serbia and invited to take an active part in the struggle against political excesses that were not conducive to 'democratic relations' between Church and state. The chairman of the Catholic Bishops' Conference was attacked for stating in Rome that the conditions in which young Catholics grow up in Yugoslavia were not such as to encourage their faith. The Catholic Church was blamed for its incapacity to ward off counter-revolutionary and nationalist infiltrators who wanted to use it against Yugoslavia's socialism and independence.

Essentially, the leadership of the League of Communists was reacting against any force that could compete with its monopoly of power. At a time when public opinion was gradually being enlightened on the legitimising myths and slogans, the regime was naturally sensitive to the manipulation of sectional feelings – the only ones that rouse crowds – by forces beyond its control. In that way it was doing homage indirectly to the role that religion continues to play, or is playing again. The authorities were thus indirectly contributing to the political importance of religion, at the same time as they were admitting the failure of their own ideological efforts.

Short of giving way to political pluralism, no Communist government in Yugoslavia is likely to want to do more for the historic religious denominations than to protect them as part of the country's cultural heritage. They can be tourist attractions, even listed museum specimens, but they must never again be allowed to become living forces in society. Man aspires to an inaccessible absolute truth, and totalitarianism, by arbitrarily raising a fragment of truth to the level of absolute certainty, can offer such an illusion. Thus all the efforts to overcome totalitarianism will make little headway in practice if they neglect its spiritual background. Luckily for the leadership of the ruling League of Communists of Yugoslavia, religion there is not a unifying force. It is not yet able to provide the sort of spiritual renewal that could overcome the false unity of totalitarianism, even though the latter has already been largely unmasked.

8

YUGOSLAVIA'S PLACE IN THE WORLD

The origins of Yugoslavia's non-alignment

General Hackett's 'Third World War' starts in Yugoslavia. To be precise, the fictional preliminaries were made to occur in July 1985 with a Soviet incursion in Slovenia, in answer to a call for help from the Soviet-sponsored Committee for the Defence of Yugoslavia. Within days, according to the General's scenario, Soviet units were in action against United States troops that had arrived from Italy (Sir John Hackett, *The Third World War – The Untold Story*, London, 1982).

From time to time, the West becomes nervous about Yugoslavia. For instance, in 1968, after the Soviet intervention in Czechoslovakia, NATO sent signals to deter the Soviet Union from any move against her. Then at the beginning of 1980, when Soviet armour had moved into Afghanistan and Tito lay dying, Western eyes were again turned on Yugoslavia. Suddenly, the land of the South Slavs was no longer the dashing and progressive leader of the Third World, but a poor and unsteady country on the other side of the Adriatic that could become a future Soviet target. News commentators said that if the Russians were tempted into what in 1968 had been called the 'grey zone of NATO', the whole strategy of the Atlantic Alliance in the Mediterranean would have to be reconsidered. The crystal ball gazers of political science and the players of international relations party games had already been indulging for some years in such speculation, and writing scenarios of intervention. They generally agreed that the great attraction for the Soviet Union in seeking to obtain control of Yugoslavia was access to her coastline.

What could NATO do to counteract a direct Soviet intervention? Only an armed attack on one of its members binds the alliance to assistance, and there is no legal basis upon which the organisation as such could operate militarily on the side of Yugoslavia. At the same time, the total security requirements of the alliance call for a broader view. Despite a reluctance to grapple with 'out-of-area' problems, it is now widely recognised that such requirements are directly affected by events beyond the NATO area. The allies could decide, individually or collectively, to extend material aid to a universally recognised government against unprovoked aggression, in answer to a request by that government. But an analysis of the forces available for the defence of the alliance in Europe, and of the ways in which such aid could be brought to Yugoslavia, reduces the probability of direct assistance rapid or massive enough to be effective.

The nearest Yugoslavia ever came to NATO was in 1953–4 when, in the wake of the Korean War, a frightened Tito reluctantly committed himself in some manner to the Western alliance, in return for protection, by associating with Greece and Turkey in the Balkan Pact. In Yugoslav eyes, however, this was merely a temporary arrangement and, within a year of Stalin's death, the pact had become a dead letter. Yugoslavia's foreign policy then became a blend of two ingredients, one emerging from Tito's longing for a bigger role, and another from his country's geopolitical position. Whereas the former was revolutionary, ideological and loudly proclaimed, the latter was traditional, pragmatic and unrecognised. As we saw in Chapter 4, non-alignment fitted into a long tradition of balance and ambivalence, which Tito would not have acknowledged.

Right from the start, the foreign policy of the Yugoslav Communists looked out ambitiously, beyond their ideological neighbourhood, to the Mediterranean and to the entire continent of Europe. As early as May 1944, Kardelj was writing, with praise from Tito: 'We must already now strive for our country to become an influential factor in the setting up of the future international order' (Vladimir Dedijer, *Novi prilozi za biografiju Josipa Broza Tita*, II, Rijeka, 1981). Five months later, on 27 October 1944, Tito said in his first speech in liberated Belgrade: 'We have acquired the right to take our place as equals with the Allies in the war, and also in the building of a new and happier world.' However, there is no real evidence of the Yugoslav Communists' 'struggle against spheres of influence' going back to 1943, as Dedijer would have us believe, just as it does not make sense to claim that they were opposed at that time to the provisions of the Yalta Conference and the arrangements that had preceded it. Dedijer's hypothesis of the 'widest coalition in the Second World War' – British plans to liquidate the Yugoslav Communist movement through the chetniks before the arrival of the Red Army, with the connivance of the Axis and the happy abstention of the Russians – points less to Anglo-American intentions than to the partisans' obsessional fears of a landing by the Western Allies, and to their distrust of the Western support that had helped them through a stage in their struggle when their survival was at stake.

At Tehran, Tito was spared the possibility of a landing in Dalmatia that he feared so much, and it was agreed there to help his movement to the greatest possible extent. By the time of the Churchill-Stalin meeting in Moscow, the Red Army was conducting joint operations with the partisans in Yugoslavia at the request of Tito, who already held most of the country. At worst, the 'fifty-fifty' deal, which had amended Molotov's 'sixty-forty' proposal, did Tito no harm; at best, it helped him. The rough equilibrium envisaged by Churchill was later to become the bulwark of Tito's non-alignment. As for Yalta, it gave Tito the opportunity to complete and formalise his control over Yugoslavia.

The Yugoslav Communists had successfully turned a war against foreign invaders into a revolutionary struggle, and brought the country solidly into the Soviet camp. They were full of self-confidence and of revolutionary dynamism. The crisis in relations with Moscow arose from Tito's ambitions outside Yugoslavia. It was difficult enough to keep any control over his domestic establishment, but this was nothing compared to the liability that the Kremlin would have to face if Tito's government succeeded in creating a vast Balkan complex which would expect to share in the formulation of overall Communist-bloc policy, and that with a naïve disregard for the realities of power at global level. The Soviets wanted to be able to control Yugoslavia more directly in view of her important strategic position and the increasing tension in Europe.

Having stood up to Moscow, Tito was eventually led by his love of power and by his desire to spread Communism to support almost any takeover bid elsewhere by a Communist, socialist or 'progressive' minority, provided it was not done with direct Soviet military involvement. In the mid 1950s, the Yugoslavs turned to ever-expanding contacts with the emerging nations of the post-colonial world. The rallying call came to be known as 'non-alignment'. Yugoslavia's ties with the Third World allowed her to weaken her links with the West, and facilitated reconciliation with the Soviet bloc on her own terms after Stalin's death. Over the 1950s and '60s, her leaders came to imagine an ideal commonwealth of equal socialist forces, with an important role for themselves in promoting 'socialism'

By the late 1950s, they had concentrated their attention on Nasser's Egypt, and from there branched out in the Arab world and the Algerian independence movement. Of the three centres of revolution and socialism vying for influence in Asia and Africa – Moscow, Peking and Belgrade – Belgrade, with its concern for national independence, was probably closest to the feelings of Afro-Asian nationalism. Tito increasingly made use of international opinion outside the blocs to appear as a world leader. The selection of Belgrade as the venue for the first non-aligned summit conference in 1961 was Yugoslavia's greatest diplomatic success; yet, even as early as that meeting, her non-alignment showed an anti-Western bias. The second conference, held in Cairo in 1964, already reflected the drawbacks of non-alignment as a united movement. Relations with France in particular deteriorated seriously over Tito's aid to the Algerian National Liberation Front. The West in general was reminded of the quintessential fact of Yugoslavia's Communism by the apparently narrowed gap between the foreign policies of Belgrade and Moscow.

Prestige diplomacy

The prestige of Yugoslavia was at its highest in the Arab Middle East, where it backed Nasser's pan-Arabism. Tito played a perceptible role during the 1967 conflict. From the start, he gave Egypt complete support, and Nasser's defeat came as a blow, for without him Yugoslav influence would be greatly reduced. Tito did everything in his power to help restore the military fortunes of the Egyptian leader by fully co-operating with, and urging on, the Soviet bloc. More realistic counsels eventually prevailed, and Tito turned towards mobilising world opinion to restore, as nearly as possible, the pre-war situation. His venture, approved by the Warsaw Pact allies, was brushed aside by Israel, and was not followed with enthusiasm by the Arabs cither.

The Yugoslavs also tried to promote non-aligned socialism on a Mediterranean scale through conferences of 'progressive' political organisations. They denounced the presence of military forces from powers not bordering on the Mediterranean, but at their 1968 Rome meeting, the 'progressives' generally preferred to limit their final declaration to calling for the exclusion of the United States and Britain, and Yugoslavia did not sign it. She took her stand on the belief that the idea of socialism was stronger in the Mediterranean than was realised by the Soviets whose military presence, far from being essential for its pro-motion, could actually compromise it. Her position was nevertheless basically anti-American: if the Mediterranean could be rid of US forces, there would be no need for Soviet forces to balance them, and socialism in the area would be able to direct its own destiny. At the same time, Yugoslavia's missionary zeal certainly helped to create an image of the Soviet Union as an outsider in the Mediterranean.

Such was Tito's way of dealing with the Soviets. When they were cordial, he was only too happy to be friendly. When they resorted to pressure, he resisted, and he made sure that the world knew about it. Yugoslavia's foreign policy in the 1960s was, on occasion, as close to that of the Soviet Union as the stand of any Warsaw Pact ally, because Soviet interests at times coincided with those of Yugoslavia. If Tito generally aligned himself with Moscow in defence of the Arab cause, it was because he was no neutral in the Middle East. The Arab cause was one of the vehicles for Tito's promotion of socialism in the Mediterranean. Independent though it was, Yugoslavia's diplomacy was that of a party leadership anxious to play a leading role in the international movement gathered around the concept of Communist socialism.

While stressing the principle of equality between Communist parties, Yugoslavia was finding more and more in common with the Soviet Union as the 1960s went on. Paradoxically, when Yugoslavia's vital interests appeared to be placed in jeopardy by the 1968 Soviet armed intervention in Czechoslovakia, she was, in fact, moving back to her previously close relationship to the Soviet Union. Having institutionalised non-alignment as Yugoslavia's constitutional foreign policy, Tito had realised that the influence of the non-aligned movement in world affairs was fast declining.

Imposed originally by circumstances, the Yugoslav diplomacy of non-alignment had reached the stage where ideology had almost completely displaced all considerations of geography, history, economics or culture. The country's rulers had come to look upon themselves as leaders of the Third World and as the main propagators of socialism there. The international role brought Yugoslavia a measure of independence, with much glamour. Tito's influence in Asia and Africa was probably one of the reasons for the attention paid him by the Soviet Union. It satisfied the vanity of the Yugoslav leadership, and ended up feeding Tito's narcissism. Yet it has to be admitted that the Third World, while admiring Yugoslavia's ability to manoeuvre between the super-powers, never paid too much attention to the actual nature of her domestic policies. It could also be argued that Yugoslavia had helped to spread Soviet influence among the non-aligned countries of the Mediterranean and Middle East, thus in a sense endangering her own position. In all this, contradictions were superficial and easy to reconcile if referred back to Titoism.

Yugoslavia went through a period of turmoil after 1967. Tito was trying to be the guide of a movement of uncommitted states; his country was looking Westward, culturally and economically, and yet ideologically it remained tied to the East. Yugoslavs felt in danger, as a result of Soviet action in Czechoslovakia, and yet the uncommitted did not raise their voices. Yugoslav non-alignment was turned into an 'anti-bloc' diplomacy. The emphasis changed to 'defending the country's independence and integrity'. The rhetoric was that the Yugoslav system offered the only genuine opposition to the two established power-blocs, each with its own sphere of influence, and neither of which had been able to improve the condition of contemporary man.

It was in 1968 that the Yugoslavs discovered their opposition to the Yalta agreement. The idea had been taken over from Gaullist France, where Yalta had become one of the symbols of the division of Europe, but it suited Yugoslavia's new stance. It also helped to curry favour with General de Gaulle. Tito had now become anxious for French support, which was less embarrassing than any American connexion. Broadly speaking, more attention was paid to Europe – not only to France but also to Italy, and eventually to all countries of the European Community. This meant (as indicated in Chapter 4) welcoming, and even attempting to lead, a loose gathering of southern European Communist parties in opposition to Soviet attempts to re-establish authority over the world Communist movement. Simultaneously, the Yugoslavs had to be careful to balance this advantage against the detrimental effects that the Eurocommunists' pluralistic approach might have on Party authority at home.

Conditions in the Balkans favoured the renewal of proposals for regional co-operation. These had first been produced as far back as 1957, in the context of a series of schemes inspired by Khrushchev for the reduction of East-West tension through the weakening of NATO. The initiative now came, in a different context, from the Greek government of Constantine Karamanlis, and led to the conference held in Athens in 1976, attended by Bulgarian, Greek, Romanian, Turkish and Yugoslav representatives. This meeting produced a long list of suggestions for co-operation in non-political areas. Yugoslavia, which had welcomed the effort, nevertheless showed considerable scepticism, reflecting fear of great-power manipulation, particularly of outstanding bilateral issues such as Macedonia, and the formal need to stress her own non-alignment. Yugoslav officials proudly maintained that their country could have no special Balkan policy, because it had a global concept of non-alignment. As one of her diplomats told an American analyst (A.Borowiec, *Yugoslavia after Tito*, New York, 1977), Yugoslavia 'has

emerged from the narrow Balkan context into the world scene as an
active participant in global affairs.'

Additionally, Tito travelled to both Greece and Turkey in 1976,
offering to mediate, and generally trying to exploit both countries' disenchantment with NATO, for the vague purpose of creating a non-
aligned Balkan zone. Whereas this could be dismissed as rhetoric, the
presence of Markos Vafiadis in Yugoslavia in the summer of 1978 surely
indicates that there was a specific Yugoslav Balkan policy. The one-time
commander of the Communist-led Democratic Army, who was to
return home from exile in 1983, had been closely connected with Yugoslavia's support of the Communists during the Greek civil war up till
1949. Could he have come on a holiday to Skopje from the Soviet Union,
where he had been living since 1950, without the approval of both the
Soviet and the Yugoslav authorities? In 1982 *Politika*, the major Yugoslav daily paper, serialised extracts from a forthcoming book by a Yugoslav Macedonian journalist, who described his encounters with 'General'
Markos in 1978. Was it to show that the Yugoslavs had not really
stabbed the Greek patriots in the back at the end of the civil war, and to
put their record straight with the new Socialist administration in
Athens – perhaps even to find favour in the eyes of the Greek Communists? Throughout the 1970s, there was also a process of 'normalisation' with Albania. If, as suggested in Chapter 6, Tito had sought to
influence Albania through the Albanian minority in Yugoslavia, he
would have been disappointed, had he lived a little longer, to see that his
policy had boomeranged.

Yugoslavia's independent status was the result of her geopolitical
situation as the Communist-ruled territory most exposed to the West, of
her own Communist movement which arose out of the civil strife in the
Second World War, and of the exceptional amount of help she received
from the West. Even the internal political consolidation that took place
during the 1970s was backed indirectly by Western financial assistance.
Yet in those days such support still could not be sought publicly, or even
acknowledged, for fear of the consequences that a Westward turn would
have on the Communists' domestic monopoly of power – even though
the main threat to the country's security since 1948 had been from the
East. The anti-bloc policy assumed the two blocs to be similar. Officially, it could not see that the West hardly formed a homogeneous unit
in its reactions to Soviet imperialism, let alone on other issues, and that
even the United States usually pursues a policy of opposition to the
extension of Soviet influence rather than an anti-Communist, or even an

anti-Soviet, policy as such. Yugoslavia still upheld the view of the United States as the enemy of socialism, and of political and social progress generally.

An independent Communist and European country, Yugoslavia ended up by posing as part of the Third World which Tito wanted to lead. She kept an allegiance to a non-alignment that had become a mythical monster and a dogma. While this policy still gratified Tito's vanity in the 1970s, it no longer offered the Yugoslav leadership anything more than a convenient way of slipping out of certain obligations towards the Communist states of Eastern Europe, and of avoiding the consequences of its ties with Western Europe.

Tito, by then, had in any event resumed his close relationship with the Soviet Union. Ideological in its essence, its ambitions and its appearance, Yugoslavia's foreign policy had been pragmatic only in its tactics. Tito had been careful to combat the impression that he had been inclined to appease Moscow. He had always managed to convey to the West his anxieties about Soviet pressures, as well as his willingness to resist them, provided the requisite degree of Western backing was forthcoming. Once he had obtained the right response, he had been quick to stress how good Soviet-Yugoslav relations were. The same behaviour was continued by his heirs at the time of his death.

Foreign policy since Tito

The Yugoslav leadership has nurtured a sense of chronic threat to the country's independence, not only from the East where it has some reality, but also from the West where Yugoslavia has few enemies. The behaviour of Tito's regime in his last years – repression of potentially anti-Soviet or pro-European elements, gratuitous display of an anti-Western stance, and significant concessions to the Soviet Union – was creating an atmosphere, at least in the United States, that was not very conducive to Western support of an imperilled post-Tito leadership.

In 1973 Rijeka was used as an embarkation point for Soviet heavy equipment going by way of Hungary to the Middle East. After that, the Soviet navy quietly increased its utilisation of Yugoslav ports, with supply and repair facilities and its own floating dry dock in the Bay of Kotor. The Soviet Union was also intermittently granted overflight privileges by Yugoslavia – including flights involved in logistical support to Egypt and Syria in 1973 and to Angola in 1976, and ongoing

Soviet reconnaissance flights on their way to the Mediterranean. In the spring of 1975, Tito told a Czechoslovak military delegation: 'Formally we are not members of the Warsaw Pact, but if the cause of socialism, of Communism, of the working class, should be endangered, we know where we stand . . . We hold our aims in common with the Soviet Union.' By the end of that year, the League of Communists had put it in writing (in the Party weekly *Komunist*, 15 December) that non-alignment was an anti-imperialist policy with a class content leading to socialism. Was Tito thereby trying to diminish the Kremlin's incentive to resort to armed force against his successors?

During some thirty years, Yugoslavia had tried to implement a global foreign policy. Tito's costly diplomacy had, up to a point, covered his country's internal problems, but it had failed to solve them. After his death, the problems were too great to be concealed any longer, and Tito was no longer there to want to do it. An uncertain or chaotic situation could thus presumably turn Yugoslavia into a Soviet target. Soviet leaders considering its occupation would nevertheless have to weigh a number of factors, such as the degree of resistance they would encounter, the need to claim that they were answering a call for help, the extent of the reliance they could place on the Warsaw Pact allies, and the nature of any reactions from the West. A direct intervention is unlikely, except as a last resort in an internal or an international crisis. But, even in that case, would the Russians risk a world crisis for a country that may well be, in global strategic terms and in a perspective that has become fluid, less important that it has been made to appear?

The Soviet leaders have come to accept that Yugoslavia is a special case. They know that its independence is considered by the West to be an important factor in international relations. They will obviously take advantage of trouble where they can, but strategically their position is defensive. They have other problems to cope with – Afghanistan and Poland among them – and they can hardly afford to turn Yugoslavia into yet another one. Even Soviet hawks would agree that the best policy is to let Yugoslavia become weaker. Closer economic ties having been achieved, pressure to obtain political and strategic concessions could be increased.

Soviet pressure could be exerted through separatists and through neighbours. Threatened with dismemberment, and having lost much freedom to manoeuvre, Yugoslavia's leadership might well want to return to the Soviet fold, and claim that Titoism had thereby been saved. The country could actually slide back into place without much drama or too many international complications. The leadership of the Communist Party of Yugoslavia, finding itself in a dilemma after 1948, managed to become free of its loyalty to the Soviet Union. Why should not the leadership of the League of Communists of Yugoslavia be able to drop non-alignment, and find its place again alongside the Soviet Union? The Russians have been active in Yugoslavia since Tito's death. Soviet interests on the Adriatic coast have been sharpened by an appreciation of the economic resources of its hinterland, while at the same time the Soviet Union is the main supplier of oil, gas and heavy military equipment. In fact, Yugoslav trade with the Soviet bloc has reached a level that gives Moscow considerable political and economic leverage.

For a year or two after Tito's death, his successors tried to maintain some semblance of a non-aligned movement abroad, at the same time as they tried to check an ever more worrying economic situation at home. They placed their undertaking under the sign of Tito's continuing posthumous presence. They continued to move around the globe, trying to keep on schedule the preparation of the non-aligned conference which was to have been held in Baghdad in 1982, wanting to mediate between Iraq and Iran, discussing the situation in Southern Africa, proclaiming their support for the Palestine Liberation Organisation (PLO) and calling for a Palestinian state, condemning Israel's 'genocide' in Lebanon, and demanding her withdrawal from all territories occupied since 1967. At their Twelfth Party Congress in 1982, they gave a prominent place to delegations from the PLO, the South West African People's Organisation (SWAPO), and the Communist parties of Italy, China, Greece and the Soviet Union. They did their best to stir up ill feelings between Athens and Tirana (after Albania's overtures to Greece), and between Ankara and Sofia (over the Turkish minority in Bulgaria). And they attacked Western governments for giving hospitality to Yugoslav opposition groups.

Inevitably all this bustle about world policy, particularly the most distant problems, was in a lower key. No longer did it have Tito to act as a resonance chamber; it sounded less convincing, and raised no interest whatsoever at home. Furthermore, the need for austerity had forced the government to reduce the cost of its sumptuous diplomacy. With her $20 billion hard-currency debt, Yugoslavia was anxious to stress that she was a non-aligned country with good borrowing habits, in whose creditworthiness the West had an obvious interest. No sooner had Tito been laid to rest in 1980 than the government introduced its first anti-inflationary measures, devaluing the dinar by 30 per cent, compressing domestic demand and wages, reducing investment, and channelling resources into exports to the West.

By the end of 1981, however, it was clear that such measures had failed to come to grips with the economic crisis. The reluctance of Western creditors to lend more caused a continued squeeze that seemed to subordinate all policies to the achievement of balance-of-payment targets. In June 1982, the government finally admitted the real situation publicly: economic recovery could not even begin without a modicum of public confidence, as Yugoslavia would have to spend more than 50 per cent of all its earnings on debt repayment due that year. The deep structural imbalances had been revealed with unexpected swiftness and intensity. After three decades of destroying the old social order and replacing it with the zigzag and stop-go 'Yugoslav way to socialism', the discrepancy between its theory and its practice had left people confused and vulnerable, and cadres bewildered and cynical.

Tito had designated the army as the bastion, not only of the country's independence, but also of its social and political order, and ever since the 1970s Yugoslavia had seen a creeping influence of the military. In 1982 and 1983 angry words were spoken on appropriate occasions by top generals, implying that the politicians were allowing the situation to get out of hand. Divisions within the leadership were giving the generals the impression that the army might be the only reliable guardian of Tito's legacy. The military is certainly the most consistent, the most conscientious and the most traditionalist keeper of that inheritance. (So much so that one Yugoslav journalist told the present author in the summer of 1982 that the military leader, if one were ever to emerge, would not be so much a Yugoslav Jaruzelski or even a Yugoslav Pinochet as a Yugoslav Tejero!*)

The uncertainty that hangs over the future has made the leadership agree on one point: to increase the defence budget, even though it finds increasing difficulty in financing such an effort, and the Yugoslav army provides more quantity than quality. The domestic arms industry supplies much of its needs, and has become a thriving exporter, for Yugoslavia is one of the top ten arms exporters and one of the big suppliers to the Third World. Yet high-technology weaponry and spare parts still have to be imported, and the essentials of its armour and aircraft come from the Soviet Union. Its equipment is ageing, standards of maintenance are poor, its backbone remains the traditional infantry

*Tejero was the officer who attempted to storm the Spanish *Cortes* in 1981.

battalion, and the training of its conscripts is largely a formal exercise. These deficiencies are covered up with the cosmetics of the General People's, or territorial, Defence – of which less and less is heard. It exists mainly on paper, in words, and to give veterans the illusion of continuing to serve Party and country.

The increased political role of the army could hamper its capability to defend the national territory against foreign aggression. The doctrine preached to all ranks is that the country is threatened by American imperialism and its pawns (occasionally identified as Italy and Austria) no less than by Soviet hegemony and its auxiliaries (often named as Bulgaria and, much more rarely, Hungary); NATO is as dangerous as the Warsaw Pact. The deterrent value of Yugoslavia's defences is obviously less than is made to appear. At best, her military efforts add up to a psychological deterrent of limited power.

The Western attitude, the Balkan alternative

Western support for Communist Yugoslavia has been anti-Soviet, a support that her leaders have shared with their Chinese opposite numbers, as well as with various monarchs, presidents, generals, colonels and other authoritarian rulers over the past thirty years. Not only does the West see no valid alternative to Titoism, even beyond the grave, but there was also much unreasonable Western admiration for what was known as 'Tito's Yugoslavia', and for the personality of the late Marshal in particular, based in part on the impression that the system he built up and bequeathed to his country is basically pro-Western.

As the price for Yugoslavia's independence from the Soviet bloc, the West has also underwritten the mismanagement of her economy. By the 1970s, bankers had become only too happy to lend in order to help recycle the massive surpluses of OPEC members, and they hardly needed political prompting. By the beginning of the 1980s, however, they found themselves in the tricky situation of having to reschedule debts to enable nearly defaulting nations to meet interest payments. The Yugoslav government, which is among the sounder of the great borrowers, managed for a while to avoid formal rescheduling, as it thought this would damage the image of the country's distinct brand of regime and policies. The rescue operation that enabled it to meet its 1983 schedule was little more than a face-saving rescheduling. It provided the Yugoslav leaders with a period of transition, after which they accepted the reality, the real words used to describe it, and even a measure of pressure from Western and international bankers.

Bankers had come to see their dilemma, caught as they were between, on the one hand, having to exert more sway over Yugoslavia's economic policies while continuing to provide credit, and on the other, having to refuse more credit and thus put existing loans at risk. The governments of the Atlantic Alliance, however, appear to face no dilemma, and give the impression that they envisage only one possible pair of alternatives: Titoism continuing without Tito, or the Soviet Union taking all. The real alternative is not one between the *status quo* and a return to the Soviet fold. It is a question of knowing which way the collective leadership will turn to make up for the authority that it has been losing rapidly since the departure of Tito, and to what extent its members are likely to agree among themselves. In spite of growing popular disenchantment with the system, and the readiness of some sections of the leadership to discuss what is wrong with the current situation, Tito's successors have so far been unable to agree on even the outlines of reform proposals.

Whether the NATO governments were right in thinking that Titoism was the best solution for Yugoslavia's relationship with the West up till the very end of Tito's reign is debatable. That they appear to see Titoism without Tito as the only hope for Yugoslavia's independence is disturbing. The *status quo* is changing. Genuine non-alignment requires support for change, in the direction of a more pluralistic system that need not be anti-Soviet. If the West does not have a clear idea of how it would like Yugoslavia to evolve, the mirage of the *status quo* will quickly fade away, because those who are prepared to defend the present order are also those who fear change, even if they sympathise with the aspirations of others who want change.

Before they have a great fall like Humpty Dumpty, and can never be put together again, they could be the first to run for help to the Soviet Union, which does not need to create problems or uphold stability, and knows how to exploit in its own interest the possibility of change in Yugoslavia. Could the leadership, even if it were united, hold out against both the Soviet Union and increased domestic dissension? There is a strong likelihood that the people in power would then let themselves be carried along by a drift that would bring the country back to the Soviet Union's side.

On the other hand, the leadership might try to obtain the confidence of a broader consensus for a more open style of government, which could pursue down-to-earth policies in an atmosphere of responsible internal debate. Tito is no longer there to prevent such a trend – to put on the brakes or go into reverse. At the very least that sort of approach would not worsen existing problems, and would not upset the established principles of the union of differentiated nationalities, of socialist self-management, or of non-alignment with existing military alliances.

The country's limited freedom of choice to evolve this way or that depends on the attitude of the international community. It would be helped by an accepted and acknowledged neutrality. It is only in conditions of relative détente that a country like Yugoslavia can keep a certain margin of independence and a limited amount of choice. The interests of East and West converge to the extent that neither would gain from her collapse in the near future. Without Tito, Yugoslavia has already had to acknowledge the limited nature of leadership in the present world. Much water has flowed under the bridge since Yugoslav diplomats boasted that she was 'an active participant in global affairs'. It should not be too difficult also to acknowledge the limited nature of her development.

Her limited freedom of choice would be helped by a more clearly businesslike Western attitude. Praise for the Titoist legacy causes contempt and an impression of insincerity. It makes Tito's successors and the population at large doubt whether the West can be relied upon, and may encourage them to seek and accept a reassurance from Moscow since Moscow is seen, on the whole, as having come to accept Yugoslavia as she is. Western policy has been inadequate in so far as it has not fully taken into account the need to maximise the prospects for positive change, and thus failed to take advantage of the opportunity to pull the rug from under Soviet feet.

In spite of blanket references by all US presidents to their interest in Yugoslavia's independence and integrity, the American approach since the mid-1970s has been altogether incoherent. President Reagan's policies do not seem to imply the danger of direct aggression in Europe, and to that extent almost leave Yugoslavia out of reckoning. As for the European partners of the Atlantic Alliance, they expressed concern at the time of Tito's death, while the European Community rushed to bring to a rapid conclusion its long-protracted trade negotiations with Yugoslavia. Do the Europeans – those of the EC – still consider that they have 'vital' interests beyond their immediate present borders? If they do, what sacrifices are they ready to make in order to sustain such interests, and to what extent does Yugoslavia figure among them?

Yugoslavia's limited freedom of choice would be enhanced if the Soviet Union knew unambiguously that the Western allies, individually and collectively, regarded her military neutrality and political independence as an essential component of the established balance of power. While they would understandably not want to limit their options in advance, committing themselves to the defence of Yugoslavia as she stands at present, it would not be in their interest that Moscow should feel more or less free to resort to arms. Yugoslavia needs some form of protection from the threat of military intervention if she is to open out rather than close in. A major factor affecting Soviet policy decisions on Yugoslavia is thus likely to be the extent of Western skills in signalling, but the West would first have to decide how much it valued Yugoslavia's ability to remain independent and neutral, and to adapt to changing circumstances.

She might be encouraged in her limited freedom of choice if it were decided that she was also worth some economic sacrifices at a time when the West feels sorry for itself. This need not mean pouring in more cash to keep afloat (or, more accurately, adrift) the blend of empty rhetoric and inefficiency, nor would it mean using trade as a negative political instrument. It could be a 'give-and-take'. In a businesslike atmosphere, no one could object to advice being given to the Yugoslav leaders on how to approach some of their problems.

Dogmatically rather than pragmatically non-aligned, Yugoslavia is dangerously isolated. Would it not suit her interests better to anchor somewhere, and to anchor where she happens to be located geographically? There are, in historical terms, several aspects of Europe other than the one that has taken shape around Western Europe. One of these is Balkan Europe, whose organic realisation is, in the foreseeable future, obviously impossible. Nevertheless, Yugoslavia could return to what Borowiec's diplomat had somewhat contemptuously called 'the narrow Balkan context'. She should not find it too difficult as an absolute neutral to hitch on to the Balkans, a region that cuts across military alliances, most of whose leaders in recent years have expressed the wish to turn the peninsula into an area of peace and co-operation, and where Yugoslavia could provide positive services by a truly neutral existence. A new Balkan connection that would underpin her independence from both blocs would be one way of ending Yugoslavia's isolation.

Her three Communist Balkan neighbours all expressed concern about the international situation at the time of Tito's death. Relations with Romania had been developing well, though never to the extent of actual military co-operation. If they have reached a point beyond which it seems they will not mature, it is because of the uncertainty each feels about the development of the other's relationship with the Soviet Union. Bulgaria holds a key position in the Balkans, because she can affect Yugoslavia through Macedonia, and because she borders on two members of NATO. Relations between Sofia and Belgrade tend to reflect the state of Soviet-Yugoslav relations, even though the current Bulgarian leadership and its policies are more original than the simplistic view of 'the Soviet Union's best satellite' would have it. We saw in Chapter 6 that, even though relations between Belgrade and Tirana are tense, there are limits to the war of words waged between them, and that both sides share two characteristics: they are insecure, and they are independent of the Soviet Union.

From the southern, NATO, side Greece has established links with her Communist neighbours – a policy actually initiated by the 'Colonels' who ruled the country in 1967–74. Worried about future developments in the peninsula, particularly in Yugoslavia, the Karamanlis government was then anxious to set up regional ties in order to help stabilise the situation. Relations improved further with the advent of a Socialist administration in Athens at the end of 1981. The two governments have pledged to keep on strengthening mutual links, and to broaden Balkan regional ideas. Papandreou's government was intent on expanding Greece's active interest in Balkan co-operation, and on promoting the idea, revived by the Greek Socialist leader, of a Balkan nuclear-free zone. This received strong support from President Zhivkov of Bulgaria, and was welcomed in all Balkan capitals except Tirana and – to the extent that Turkey is also a Balkan country – Ankara. The Turks too have had a round of talks and visits with Balkan Communist governments, including Yugoslavia.

The nuclear-free zone is essentially a Greco-Bulgarian project, to which Yugoslavia has responded cautiously. She has reservations about a Balkan summit devoted to it. She has argued rhetorically that such a project did not stand a chance, unless it was taken in the context of European security in general and of Mediterranean security in particular, and, more realistically, as long as bilateral issues, such as her own dispute with Bulgaria over Macedonia, remained open.

Yugoslavia and Greece have maintained close military contacts ever since the restoration of a parliamentary government in Athens, but their nature and frequency have mainly been kept secret, so determined has Belgrade been to remain, and be seen to remain, non-aligned. The Yugoslav Communists' only reservation regarding the electoral victory of the Greek Socialists was the original anti-NATO platform of PASOK. Far from wishing Greece to move away from the alliance, the Yugoslav government in the post-Tito period has been eager to see her again firmly within it. Greece in NATO discourages the Soviet Union from taking risks in the Balkans. And with Italy, she is also seen as a lifeline for material support in case of need.

The Yugoslavs are as interested as the Atlantic allies in restraining the Soviets. Their government may be coming to realise that, in an unstable situation, systematic anti-Americanism is harmful to their country, and that the European Community should occasionally be taken more seriously as an advocate of pan-European interests whose links with Yugoslavia can perform an important function to counteract her isolation. At the same time, the partners of the Atlantic Alliance could come to realise the need to save the Yugoslav regime from its own self while the situation is still fluid. If the Soviet Union is not to take all when the changes set in, it is high time to go beyond the simple view that the only interest of the West in Yugoslavia as an 'out-of-the-area' country is to prevent her from sliding back into the Soviet camp. The end it wants to prevent could, in fact, be brought nearer by toeing the Yugoslav line.

Would the Atlantic Alliance, at the very least, not want to help the survival of the present system in Yugoslavia, which had become more sound in its economics, more acceptable politically to its subjects, more adaptable to change, in short more viable in a long-term perspective that looked at the continuity of the national entity rather than at the specifics of the regime, and at its sclerotic, static, corrupt and worn-out *status quo*?

9

FROM LEGITIMATION TO DEMYSTIFICATION – FORTY YEARS OF HISTORIOGRAPHY

In Tito's time

It was in 1968 that J.H.Plumb gave the series of lectures in New York that were to become *The Death of the Past* (London, 1969). Had he done so two decades later, and had he looked at the directions taken by Yugoslav historiography from the end of the Second World War, he would have found there a good example of the 'past' as a 'created ideology with a purpose, designed to control individuals, or motivate societies, or inspire classes', 'to dictate what a man should do or believe'. He would also have found increasing evidence of historians trying to 'cleanse' the story of their country 'from those deceiving visions of a purposeful past', and who, while not being 'free from either moral or political judgments', were doing their 'best to form both in the light of history', in the belief that 'any process which increases man's awareness of himself, that strengthens his chance of controlling himself and his environment, is well worth pursuing'.

It was obvious that, in the years immediately following the end of the war and the advent of Communism, historiography in Yugoslavia would be made to serve the revolution and the construction of socialism. History was then made to begin when the Communist Party went over to the resistance in 1941. All the rest was prehistory leading to that event. Nevertheless, even in those revolutionary times, there was not much discontinuity in the old academies of Belgrade, Zagreb and Ljubljana, where real scholarship had sought a refuge from ideological upheavals.

That initial period accordingly produced different kinds of historical works. Byzantine and medieval studies, which had already reached a high level of scholarship before the war, survived well enough. At the same time, the effects of Marxism were not consistent. The interest in economic and social history thus created initiated a new exploration of the Ottoman period. For the western provinces, it produced a new insight into the Reformation, the peasant risings, the events of 1848–9.

129

The nearer it drew in time, however, the more historiography divided and less interesting it became. It appeared as Marxist positivism, drawing its inspiration from the 'scientific' experience of Marxism-Leninism and verging on propaganda, or as plain positivism, claiming to be after nothing but the facts, according to the precepts of the Rankean school, and looking somewhat outmoded.

With the turn of the 1950s to the '60s, the nineteenth century resumed its rightful place, and the end of the 1960s witnessed the first critics of the anthropological and apologetic nature of Marxist positivism in historiography. Things then began to move at a brisker pace. For a start, the rate of publication increased rapidly, particularly for the history of the inter-war period. The 1960s were also the years when the nationalism of regions and ethnic communities found its way back into old moulds. The political leadership of most of the federated units felt it imperative to turn to the past, where they looked for models that could give them a lineage. Chapter 5 has sketched out how the Communist Party came to recognise more and more national groups, so as to give satisfaction to some of them, reduce the strength of others, and end up by dealing with smaller and more manageable communities.

The fact that the encouragement given to nationalities was in inverse ratio to their size and age had its consequences in historiography. Everywhere a concern to defend or to develop one's historical identity was apparent, but real nationalist legitimation through historiography was, above all, to be found in Macedonia. Right from the start it was deemed necessary in that southern republic to bring out a specifically Macedonian history, a history that was well differentiated from that of neighbouring nations. Very early the ground had been prepared for the development of the history of the newly-recognised Macedonian nation. Its historiography not only produced an understandable plethora of monographs on the later modern period, along with an attempt at a general survey, but research into the 'ethnogenesis' of the Macedonian nation going back to the ninth century. In Montenegro, too, there was a campaign aimed at promoting a separate identity – separate from the Serbian identity that its inhabitants had traditionally shared with the inhabitants of Serbia.

By contrast, Serbian, Croatian and Slovenian schools of history appeared (and still appear) to have common characteristics – due to a different cultural climate, exchanges between scholars, a greater detachment from political contingencies, and an increasingly sophisticated methodology. The influence of new French methods was felt along with that of a more refined Marxist analysis, but events generally continued to have pride of place over structures, theoretical considerations being secondary. Where the Serbian and the Croatian identity overlapped, the recent history of Bosnia and Herzegovina also attracted scholars. It is here that one must note an important work, important both for Yugoslav historiography and for its author (no less than for the historiography of the origins of the First World War) – Vladimir Dedijer's *Sarajevo 1914* or, to give it the title of its English-language edition, *The Road to Sarajevo.* *

A massive book (1,060 pages in its first Yugoslav edition, increased to 1,354 in the second), published in 1966, it marks a change in the role played by this Yugoslav celebrity who, up till the downfall of Djilas, had been one of the heads of the Party's agitprop section and Tito's authorised biographer. It also emphasised a modification of the treatment of its subject-matter. A characteristic blend of Balkan nationalism and vaguely populist, almost libertarian Marxism had led Dedijer to concentrate on economic and social conditions in Bosnia and Herzegovina, and to place the origins of the Sarajevo conspiracy back at their source – the revolutionary youth of the two provinces. Dedijer's nationalist Marxism and his lack of proper historical training explain the innumerable prejudices and misinterpretations of detail to be found in his book. Nevertheless, they have not influenced the trend of the research. The author has not been blinded by his prejudices. His work on Sarajevo, excessively long though it is, remains a fundamental reinterpretation, and one that is essential for a proper understanding of the causes of the First World War.

There came the years when the events of the Great War and of the unification of Yugoslavia were half-a-century old, and when these topics were taken up seriously by a whole school of historians. The inter-war period was next to come into focus. There were valuable studies on the economic history of the 'First Yugoslavia', a series of monographs on the

---

*   V.Dedijer, *The Road to Sarajevo* (New York, 1966; London, 1967). Other works referred to in this chapter are, in order of appearance: Dedijer, *Novi prilozi . . .*, II (1981: with 1,262 pages of text and 80 of illustrations, it weighs 2.1 kg; vol. I was but the history of his earlier biography of Tito, vol. III was to come out in 1984; and a fourth one is planned); K.Čavoški and V.Koštunica, *Party Pluralism or Monism – Social Movements and Political Systems in Yugoslavia, 1944–1949* (New York, 1985); M.Milić, *Radjanje Titove despotije – prilog fenomenologiji jugoslovenske revolucije* (London, 1985); B.Kočović, *Žrtve Drugog svetskog rata u Jugoslaviji* (London, 1985); V.Djuretić, *Saveznici i jugoslovenska ratna drama* (Belgrade, 1985); M.Leković, *Martovski pregovori 1943* (Belgrade, 1985).

history of political parties, and a team of diplomatic historians were at work on the international relations of the Kingdom of Yugoslavia. Only the Communist Party seemed to remain in the hands of copywriters appointed by the apparatus.

In turn, even the study of the Second World became more interesting. The publication of sources gathered speed, notably in the collection of sources for the history of the People's Liberation War which extended to some 180 volumes, along with numerous local chronicles and mono-graphs, and the memoirs of revolutionary personalities reaching retire-ment age. Getting to the end of the 1960s, historians of the war, the authors of 'authorised' interpretations of the resistance to foreign occupation were venturing to suggest that in 1941 two resistance move-ments had been formed – that led by Mihailović, and that organised by the Communist Party, the former being the movement of the pro-Western bourgeoisie. Others tackled the question of the 'left-wing deviations' (or Communist 'excesses') in that same year which caused the revolution to 'stagnate' thereafter in certain regions. In 1971–2, there were round-table discussions in Belgrade and Zagreb, taken up in the press, where individual historians aired critical considerations of the 'sclerosis' of the official historiography of the Second World War.

Tito's off-the-cuff statement in 1972 that 'it was well and truly a civil war, but [that] we did not want to admit it at the time, because it would have been detrimental to our cause', already quoted in Chapter 3, could even earn him the title of father of a certain revisionism in the history of the war in Yugoslavia. During his last years, one could sense a growing interest being taken in that traumatic period. People wanted to find out what had been kept hidden. They wanted to grasp the extraordinary complexity of a complex period. They wanted to know what had hap-pened in those years that had given birth to the Communist regime. They wanted to learn about themselves. And they were afraid that they might be on the threshold of a similar period, when the equilibrium could again be broken.

At the time of Tito's death, this was expressed, on a more general level, by a public curiosity concerning sources of collective identity. A great synthesis of the *History of the Serbian Nation* to 1918 began to appear in 1981. This is the best of such ventures so far, although its Croatian counterpart has not yet been undertaken. Simultaneously, a second cam-paign endeavoured to give the Montenegrin identity a more ancient pedi-gree, going as far back as the eleventh century. This is a not uncommon Balkan characteristic – of wanting to single out one's own national group by raising it above the Slav tide, with the help of a genealogy going back to conquerors who came from Asia, or to autocthonous pre-Slav populations. In Yugoslavia, historians with fascist tendencies had already tried it in the 1930s and during the war by turning Croats into Goths. Whether they looked to tribes originating in the Caucasus or to the Veneti, such fanciful theories did not stray beyond the periphery of official historiography and of regional establishments. Reputable historians rejected them altogether.

The public finds them entertaining, but what it has wanted since Tito's death is recent history, what is called in Paris the 'history of the present time' – that overturns all taboos. Feelings of instability and fears for the future have led to great interest in the decade of the 1940s, as if to draw lessons from it for the crisis of post-Titoism. A whole range of writers exists to satisfy, or exploit, the public demand. At the bottom end, there are the hired scribblers who follow instructions imparted by the political authorities about what topics must be written up, and with the right interpretations. At the top end, there were solid, professional historians who hid behind the narrative of uncontroversial 'facts', without analysis of causes or consequences, who piled detail upon detail without ever going into essentials, who dared not question (and did not even consider) the legitimacy conveyed by the ideology of the People's Liberation War. In fact, one can say that revisionism had already got going at that level towards the end of the 1970s with such 'neo-positivist' scholars, particularly those of Zagreb who studied the Croatian side of the problem. They produced detailed, factual monographs, devoid of analysis but displaying their sources in the narrative itself, without hiding anything.

Since Tito

At a time when professional historians were too unscholarly, shy or unimaginative to raise questions or express opinions, it was outside their ranks that writers, at the beginning of the 1980s, first blurred the neat divide between black and white, in works of literature on civil war themes. They looked to the history of the 1940s to attempt a collective psychotherapy. Their novels and plays were well received by a public who knew the past half-century only through tendentious textbooks or through the legends propagated loudly by the winners, but also and increasingly, even if *sotto voce*, by the losers. The authorities reacted by accusing these writers of insulting the revolution, raising the ghosts of nationalism and denying the class character of the partisan movement; it asked the jaded question: 'Who is behind all this?' But these works sought first and foremost to probe further, to raise questions, to stop blaming proverbial bogeymen and 'seek the blame in ourselves' (as a character in one of the novels said), to know what really happened so that it should never happen again. Behind them, there was neither counter-revolution nor the secret services of foreign powers, as the press liked to stress – merely a mood that was characteristic of the time.

That mood was favourable to Dedijer's bomb, the second volume of his *New Contributions to a Biography of Josip Broz Tito* which opened up yet a new chapter in the author's career, as well as a new phase in the evolution of Yugoslav historiography. In an indigestible hotchpotch of prejudices and stage whispers, of historical footnotes and fundamental issues, the one-time chronicler of the revolution relates how the history of the war has often been doctored – by the secret police, Party leaders and Tito himself. He makes revelations on the links between Yugoslav Communists and the Soviet Union; on the difficulties encountered with separatist nationalists among the Communists in Croatia, Macedonia and Kosovo; on quarrels between Yugoslavia's Communist leaders; on the brutality of summary executions by the partisans, within their own ranks as well as among their enemies; on their contacts with Mihailović's men although the latter were, in Tito's words, 'our main opponents, now and for the future'; on their links with the Ustashas and with the Germans. The book caused a furore; it raised the wrath of partisan veterans and politicians, and attracted the curiosity of a host of more general readers.

A Western reader, even one familiar with such lengthy biographies as Martin Gilbert's *Churchill* or Renzo De Felice's *Mussolini*, would be taken aback by the structure of Dedijer's *Tito*. The author himself wrote barely a third of it. The rest is made up of 'contributions' by other people, of interviews, conversations, documents and photographs, all jumbled together. Endlessly repetitive, indifferent to evidence that does not favour the author's theories, quoting its sources at best in a cavalier fashion and at worst in the mysterious ways of books about spies, this is a tool historians will not find easy to handle.

Tito appears to have had a soft spot for 'Vlado' Dedijer, who always retained his sympathy and protection. He thus had access to all archives, including Tito's own papers, and help was forthcoming for his research from many important political and military personalities of the Yugoslav establishment. Was it only out of deference to the life president? Were people under the impression that Dedijer was preparing a book against Djilas? Of all Tito's one-time lieutenants, Djilas is certainly the one who received the most severe treatment in Dedijer's book, but very few of the old guard emerge unscathed from the 'New Contributions'.

What were Dedijer's intentions? He wanted to uncover Tito the great man who had been hidden under Tito the monument. This he would do by looking at him through the prism of the masses' revolutionary struggle. Like his 1914, his 1941 is set firmly among the people. He tells us that like Michelet, whom he admires, he writes history *d'en bas*, but whereas the Frenchman had but one hero – the people – his self-proclaimed Yugoslav counterpart has two heroes, the people and the great man. Like Michelet, Dedijer accepts the greatness of the revolution with all its mistakes and horrors. (The historian of the French Revolution might have accepted the Yugoslav revolution, but he would certainly not have accepted Tito.) With his filial but obsessional attempt to reassess the father of the revolution, Dedijer had started a veritable process of demystification. This noisy, emotional and maverick historiographer, who became a semi-dissident before he was turned into a historian of sorts by his election to the Serbian Academy, symbolises the mood of anxious reappraisal of the past. Characteristically, he boasted that history would never be the same again.

Having been given the right to reply to his critics in *Politika* – the paper on whose staff he had been before the war – he conceded that the form of his book was unsatisfactory, but that in its substance it contained nothing but the truth. The revolution was so great an achievement that its blemishes could be acknowledged. 'Was it not better', he asked, 'that we should tell the truth about ourselves than leave it to our enemies to do so?' Anyway, 'I am convinced that, after this book of mine, after so much lightning and thunder, the history of the revolution will have to be written in a new manner' (13 March 1982).

Dedijer's 'New Contributions' were a challenge to the professional historians, to those who shelter behind power, faith, fact, myth or tradition. Were they going to be shamed into taking it up? Not quite yet. The first to follow him were not strictly historians. Kosta Čavoški and Vojislav Koštunica were research fellows in Belgrade, respectively at the Institute of Comparative Law and the Institute of Sociology. Their book on *Social Movements and Political Systems in Yugoslavia, 1944–1949* is a study of the techniques used by the Communist Party to eliminate what remained of independent political groups that had survived the war.

Published by the Institute of Social Sciences of the University of Belgrade in 1983, it was banned, but subsequently appeared in English in the United States.

Miodrag Milić's essay on *The Making of Tito's Despotism* (subtitled 'Contribution to a Phenomenology of the Yugoslav Revolution') was the outcome of private seminars that had met regularly for some years in the homes of various Belgrade intellectuals to discuss topics of recent history. Djilas had been invited to one of these seminars in the spring of 1984, when the police broke in and siezed the manuscript. Milić is an intellectual who has dabbled in many areas of activity – as a scriptwriter and an amateur historian who became interested in the dynamics of the Yugoslav revolution. His thesis is that the Stalinist character of the Communist Party of Yugoslavia was the reason for its failure in Serbia and in the eastern provinces in 1941–2, because a dogmatic frame of mind wanted to clamp the Soviet model over a spontaneous popular rising. According to him, the intrinsic character of the Yugoslav revolution only showed up after 1948, but disappeared again with Djilas's fall, when the regime became a crude police-state. The manuscript led to a great political trial in the winter of 1984–5 which turned against the government, set the intelligentsia against the authorities, and divided the leadership. The author started to serve his gaol sentence in July 1986. His book appeared in London in 1985 in Serbo-Croatian, under the imprint of an expatriate publisher.

The most learned publishing firms and the Academy of Sciences in Belgrade joined in the fun. Two Belgrade enterprises competed at the beginning of 1985 to re-issue the complete works of the historian Slobodan Jovanović (1864–1958). These were classics of the history of nineteenth-century Serbia, but had never been reprinted after the war because of their author's political role. A universally respected and influential academic, Jovanović had been prime minister of the Yugoslav government in exile during the Second World War. Sentenced *in absentia* after the liberation, he had died in London. A plaque on the wall of a small hotel in Cromwell Road preserves the memory of his quiet British exile, and his remains are buried in Kensal Green cemetery under a monument that lists his scholarly achievements. There was a storm of protests from Party forums and activists until the project was given up, on the grounds of copyright difficulties.

On Dedijer's initiative, the Serbian Academy addressed itself to an awkward and controversial task: to try and work out as precise an estimate as possible of Yugoslavia's war victims, in particular the victims of

the attempted Ustasha genocide of the Orthodox Serbs in the satellite
state of Croatia. The official figure, given soon after the end of the war
and hurriedly computed for reparations purposes, was 1,706,000, which
included all the victims without dividing them into categories. Priding
itself on leading the country which, relative to its total population, had
suffered the highest number of dead in the struggle against fascism after
Poland, the Yugoslav government had, at the same time, drawn a veil
over the details so as not to open up incompletely-healed wartime
wounds, and inflame intercommunal relations. Serbian and Croatian
mythologists, however, had gladly carried on from where the authorities
had stopped. The climax of the affair was reached when two
generals – retired partisans who had become war historians, the Croat
Tudjman and the Serb Terzić – in turn broached the subject. Tudjman
gave a ridiculously reduced estimate for Serbian losses, and Terzić an
incredibly exaggerated one.

The 1940s demystified

And then came Kočović. A statistician and lawyer who had settled in
Paris, Bogoljub Kočović had also worked, quite independently and
differently, on the general question of the *Victims of the Second World
War in Yugoslavia*. Published in London in that same year 1985, his book
took everyone by surprise. The Yugoslav authorities, the academicians,
the Serbian and Croatian number-crunchers who operated on the principle 'the more the better' as though reality had not been bad enough,
were all stunned. Kočović's methodology did not consist in rummaging
through mass graves, but in a computer analysis of census returns and
demographic indices. His book was made up of a cold set of tables, with
comments and tentative conclusions. Indeed, it contained almost more
figures than words, and was totally devoid of rhetoric. It broke down the
losses into territorial and ethnic categories, and distinguished between
the broader demographic losses – about two million (dead, net emigration, and shortfall in births) – and the actual war dead – just over one
million (or between 99,000 and 1,150,000 by allowing a margin of
error).

In émigré circles, the war dead went up to three million and more,
Serbs and Croats adding relentlessly to their respective losses, the better
to accuse one another and the partisans jointly. The story completed a
full circle when the expert who had established the official figure (now

professor of Mathematics at an American university) came up to explain everything. The data he had been able to provide, in the limited amount of time allotted to him, were a rough estimate of total demographic losses. According to him, they were then presented as effective losses by the Yugoslav government in order to obtain bigger reparations. (The story was published by him in the Yugoslav dissident monthly, *Naša reč* of London, October 1985.) In June 1985, five months after the publication of Kočović's study, the Academy announced in its turn that official figures had been swollen, and that its own revised estimate of the number of actual victims of the war was between 1,100,000 and 1,500,000.

At the same time, another shot was being fired from that same institution, as though to show that Dedijer had been right in saying that history could no longer be the same – the two tomes of Veselin Djuretić's *The Allies and the Yugoslav War Drama*. The shot turned out to have a delayed charge, for nothing happened over the summer. Reactions got under way in September and, after two months of a violent campaign through meetings and the media, up and down the country, the author was expelled from the League of Communists along with his two readers. (Before being able to accept a manuscript, a Yugoslav publisher has to obtain a positive report from two acknowledged specialists who also enjoy the confidence of the Party. Their names then appear on the frontispiece of the book.) Their specific misdeeds were stated to be 'historical libel and ideological deviation'. They were also accused generally of Serbian nationalism, scientific provocation and anti-Communist propaganda.

Djuretić interprets the civil war as a conflict between two realisms – the 'existential realism' of Mihailović's movement, and the 'revolutionary realism' of Tito's. The latter eventually outmatched its opponents because it managed to manoeuvre the various ethnic communities out of the impasses into which they had been trapped by the Nazis – but not before much hoodwinking of the Western Allies, and not without much Soviet support. His interpretation is obviously a Serbian reaction, in the mood of the Serbian malaise of the 1980s, and the author places his analysis within the context of the tragic situation of the Serbian people during the time of the multiple enemy occupation. No less obviously, he exaggerates the importance of external factors, of London and Moscow. Moreover, his whole enterprise is wrapped up in contorted Marxist-style forms, peppered with philosophical considerations, and perversely long-winded. His two volumes are a difficult read.

Why did they not attract an immediate condemnation? The Belgrade apparatchiks must have had problems in going through them during the long hot summer of 1985. Besides, Djuretić was a trusted professional historian. He had been a member of the team toiling on the large-scale project of Tito's complete works at the Institute of Contemporary History in Belgrade, before passing to the Institute of Balkan Studies of the Serbian Academy. Enjoying Dedijer's protection, he had been published by the Academy, and for the first time the research institutes and the publishing enterprises did not give way to the barrage of fire from the authorities that finance them. Not only did Djuretić not lose his job, but the Belgrade Academy refused to join the chorus of condemnations.

It is unfair to say that Djuretić's book is pro-chetnik, or even anti-partisan, but it is definitely a radical reappraisal of Mihailović's movement, which is shown to be just as anti-Axis, or 'anti-fascist', as Tito's. His work is the first one on the Yugoslav revolution to appear in Yugoslavia that does not make use of the ideological prism of the Communist Party, or formulate a general indictment against all the enemies of the revolution. 'Shall we not soon have to set up a Committee for the Protection of the Revolution?' was the ironic comment of the historian Dušan Biber, who has dissected Djuretić's heavy-going prose in order to find in it as many errors as possible.

Questioning accepted interpretations and probing into myths is part of the general mood of intellectuals and readers alike. Challenges and doubts correspond to the deeper aspirations of a new generation that has overcome the polarisations, fostered by the war, of their elders. The new generation wants to know why it is that all political families and all ethnic groups have their secrets, all of which are more or less shameful, yet also more or less explicable. It has come to demand publicly that the posthumous perpetuation of the civil war be brought to an end, and it places that demand in the wider framework of its aspiration to the enjoyment of a pluralist system.

The authorities have been responding in different ways. In a solemn speech at Belgrade University at the end of 1985, General Ljubičić, a member of the collective Presidency of the Republic, issued this warning:

We cannot tolerate, and shall not tolerate, anyone who stands in our way by propagating various nationalisms, or variations on the theme of bourgeois ideology, or so-called alternatives to our system . . . There can be no ideological or political neutrality, in science, or in culture, or in education.

In line with the general's warning, and *pour encourager les autres*, a professor at the University of Novi Sad was given a prison sentence of sixty days for an article he had published earlier that year in a Belgrade weekly; in it he had taken up the theme of national reconciliation, already aired by a colleague in Slovenia. This was accompanied throughout 1986 by a general campaign of official speeches and inspired articles, taking their cue from Ljubičić's statement against 'Dedijerist' historians and writers who wanted a 'new interpretation of history'. The year ended characteristically with the banning of a new, private edition of Djuretić's book.

A different response, however, was a slim volume, published in December 1985, on 'The March 1943 Talks'. This, at long last, was the authorised interpretation of the contacts between Tito and the Germans – those contacts which for so long had been a state secret. Its author, Mišo Leković, also belonged to the team of trusted professional historians working on Tito's war memoirs. He had been entrusted more particularly with the task of preparing the material for the 'March talks', which Tito himself would have used in the memoirs that were never completed. Leković's monograph is an answer to the various interpretations given abroad, all considered to be tendentiously devaluing the importance of the People's Liberation War. It justifies the official silence, maintained up till then in Yugoslavia, on the grounds that not all the sources had previously been made accessible. White admitting that the initiative had been Tito's, it too still limits its intentions to getting the Germans to recognise the partisans as regular combatants. However, it does acknowledge the climate in which all three contenders in that triangular war (Axis, Tito, Mihailović), in expectation of a British landing, were trying to safeguard their interests and jockeying for position at each other's expense.*

---

*   There is by now an ample literature on the 1943 negotiations between partisans and Germans in Croatia, both the so-called 'March talks' and those that followed on Italy's withdrawal. The first to broach the topic of the talks on joint action, each on the basis of his own sources, were Stephen Clissold (*Whirlwind – An Account of Marshal Tito's Rise to Power*, London, 1949), Wilhelm Hoettl (originally under the pseudonym of Walter Hagen, *Die geheime Front – Organisation, Personen und Aktionen des Deutschen Geheimdienstes*, Linz and Vienna, 1950, then in the English edition under his own name, *The Secret Front – The Story of Nazi Espionage*, London, 1953), and General Rudolf Kiszling (*Die Kroaten*, Graz and Cologne, 1956).

Djilas alluded to them in his *Conversations with Stalin* (New York, 1962, and London, 1963), where he limited himself to saying that the essence of the talks lay in getting the Germans to recognise the rights of partisans as combatants. In the 1960s, the former Yugoslav diplomat Ilija Jukić (*Pogledi na prošlost, sadašnjost i budućnost hrvatskog naroda*, London, 1965) and the Yugoslav-Canadian historian

All in all, history as a discipline has not suffered too much from the attempts of Tito's regime to place it at its service. In a country as complex as Yugoslavia, whose rulers could not invent for themselves a past that went further back than the beginnings of Communism, even less could they make it go further back than the beginnings of the Yugoslav idea. They were particularly hampered by the fact that the Communist Party of Yugoslavia had long campaigned for the break-up of what Moscow considered to be an artificial creation of the Versailles settlement of Europe. They could neither take up again a unitary Yugoslav nationalism, which was associated with the monarchy and which they had already rejected, nor allow their decentralised regional offshoots to commit themselves too much to sectional nationalist schools of history.

However, they could insist on an authorised interpretation of the People's Liberation War, the legitimising factor *par excellence*, and they did so. Such a dogmatic approach was indeed successful, but it succeeded in dividing the Yugoslavs. It turned them away from all that could emphasise the historic importance and moral value of the partisans' resistance. By changing debates into trials, it inflamed passions instead of soothing them.

Yugoslavia does not need to invent a past for herself, not even a recent past. (Indeed, this has to a certain extent been shown in another book published in Belgrade at the end of 1985, by the editorial centre of

---

Ivan Avakumović (*Mihailović prema nemačkim dokumentima*, London, 1969) reconstituted the talks on the basis of German diplomatic and military records.

Because Phylis Auty, Tito's British biographer, nevertheless maintained that it had merely been a truce to exchange prisoners, Tito and his 'chief negotiator' having categorically and personally confirmed this to her (letter to the *Times Literary Supplement*, 27 November 1970), I thought it useful to sum up the then available evidence in my 'Nations of the Modern World' *Yugoslavia* (London and New York, 1971). The American historian Walter Roberts subsequently caused a diplomatic incident in 1973 by devoting a whole section of his book (*Tito, Mihailović and the Allies, 1941-1945*, New Brunswick, N.J.) to this episode.

Djilas then decided to give his interpretation in 1977 (*Wartime*, London and New York), whereas the retired ambassador General Velebit did no more than tell a Yugoslav journalist, who was writing a book on Tito's ambassadors, that his participation in the talks had been 'rather technical', in a context that was not dishonourable (D.Stuparić, *Diplomati izvan protokola*, Zagreb, 1978). He did not come back to it in his later memoirs (*Sećanja*, Zagreb, 1983). In the second volume of his 'New Contributions', Dedijer included a full chapter on the talks, using the German documents that Roberts had already revealed, the Yugoslav documents where Avakumović had read between the lines, and completely new Yugoslav eyewitness accounts, notably from Generals Koča Popović and Velimir Terzić.

Komunist. The Slovenian Communist historian Janko Pleterski, in *Nacija, Jugoslavija, revolucija* ['Nation, Yugoslavia, Revolution'], identifies with reasoned arguments based on a classical Marxist methodology, without passion or polemic, the historical processes which led the various parts to the realisation of Yugoslav unity.) It would be sufficient not to hide her past, although such freedom might reveal a past that would not necessarily conform to the tired dogmas of authority.

History understood as an intellectual process demands free research, free expression and free debate; it then runs the risk of becoming reasoned history. In Yugoslavia, over the last few years, its tendencies have been more demystifying than legitimising. They are even becoming more concerned with posing questions than with establishing the foundations of Yugoslavia's nations – at least at the level of history conceived as an intellectual process that contributes to the life of the spirit, whatever it may be at the level of officialese. Will that officialese, what the French call *la langue de bois*, suffice to hold back the questions raised by the historiography of the last half century, which undermines the legitimising foundations of the Party, and which now asserts that it is by coming to terms with its past that a society transcends it? To quote Plumb again,

The death of the past can only do good as long as history flourishes. Above all, one hopes that the past will not rise phoenix-like from its own ashes to justify again, as it so often has, the subjection and exploitation of men and women, to torture them with fears, or to stifle them with a sense of their own hopelessness. The past has only served the few; perhaps history may serve the multitude.

Mišo Leković has at long last given an authorised interpretation. Since then, a book by an investigative journalist appeared, also in Belgrade, in 1987, with an epilogue by the military historian General Milan Basta, based on new evidence from the papers of the 'German plenipotentiairy general in Croatia', Glaise von Horstenau (V.Kazimirović, *NDH u svetlu nemačkih dokumenata i dnevnika Gleza fon Horstenau, 1941–1944*), which extends the topic for the first time to the autumn of 1943.

As for the episode, referred to in chapter 3, of contacts with chetnik captains in July 1943, I have pieced it together from Italian military intelligence intercepts of radio communications. The article appeared in *Naša reč* (January 1979), which is widely read in Belgrade dissident circles, in the (apparently vain) hope that it would elicit reactions from surviving participants on both sides. Thus, almost thirty years after Clissold's account, the full story had not yet been told – at least not from the Yugoslav side.

10

CONCLUSION

Economic crisis and popular responses

On 4 April 1987, it was learnt from an item in the Riviera daily *Nice-Matin* that it had still not been possible to find a buyer for Tito's 16-cabin yacht, even though the price had been brought down to 4 million French francs. The Yugoslavs were in deep trouble, with a severe liquidity problem. Since 1985 their economy has been slowly grinding to a halt. Seventh in the league table of great debtor countries, just after Chile, Yugoslavia had managed to reduce her debt from over $21 billion in 1981 to just over $20 billion in 1984, before moving up again. The dinar, which had been depreciated by 21 per cent in 1981, by 38 in 1982, and by 75 in 1983, had fallen by no more than 50 per cent in 1984. However, by 1985 it had lost 78 per cent of its value again, 73 in 1986, and 49 in just the first half of 1987.

Similarly inflation, which had come down to a mere 50 per cent at the end of 1984, was up to 70 per cent a year later, and had reached 100 per cent at the end of 1986. By the beginning of December 1987, it was at 170 per cent, and Yugoslav economists feared that it could reach 200 per cent by the end of the year. The number of unemployed had risen to 17 per cent of the workforce. Real wages had fallen by 50 per cent in 1986 alone. Life was becoming harder with every day that passed. The IMF, the World Bank and the OECD were scathing about the Yugoslav government's failure to implement its 1983 'stabilisation' plan.

Belgrade resorted to the veiled threat that, without better terms, it could be forced to rely more heavily on the East. The industrialised countries of the West are the only ones where Yugoslavia can earn hard currency; they are her main suppliers of technology; and almost all her external debt is with the West, where she is forced to turn time and again for debt relief. Lately, she has also accumulated trade surpluses with the Soviet Union as a consequence of the falling value of Soviet raw materials. Having said that, Yugoslavia has certainly become increasingly dependent on Comecon in the 1980s, the $20 billion debt crisis accelerating a process that had started in the 1970s. By 1985 50 per cent of Yugoslavia's exports went to Comecon countries, and 35 per cent of

143

her imports came from them, with the Soviet Union itself the largest individual trading partner and major supplier of oil, gas and other crucial raw materials. Trade with Comecon countries is conducted by bilateral barter. Semi-manufactured and manufactured products are exchanged for important raw materials. The Soviet Union thus obtains from Yugo-slavia many products that can only be manufactured with imports from OECD countries, to the point where it could be said that her principal usefulness to the Russians is now as a channel for technological innova-tions from the West – with the added bonus that they do not have to be paid for in hard currency.

Having tightened as much as it could, with modest results obtained in 1984, the Yugoslav government let go again.. As productivity stagnated, its declared policies, particularly on realistic interest and exchange rates, and on tougher anti-inflation measures, were not implemented. If inter-national lenders were critical, Yugoslav economists were even harsher. Their strictures, no longer reserved for the eyes and ears of other econo-mists, were spread out in the national press during the summer of 1987. The rescheduling had merely been a wasteful and expensive buying of time, they said, for it had not been used to carry out any structural change. Political regional interests had combined to stall effective reform to liberalise the economy and open up the internal market. Since the Constitution of 1974 (the fourth and most verbose of Communist Yugo-slavia) the prerogative of central government had been reduced to national defence, foreign affairs, certain limited economic policies, and the overall maintenance of the constitutional system. But even in these federal areas, policies could be adopted and implemented only through a consensus of the local leaderships.

In order to anticipate IMF demands, a tougher stand was taken in 1987. Legislation was introduced to close loss-making enterprises, and link wage increases to productivity. Of all enterprises, 20 per cent had worked at a loss during 1986. If strictly applied, the bankruptcy law would have added between 600,000 and one million people to the one million already officially unemployed. Effective from 1 July, it was in fact applied only selectively, a few well-chosen closures serving as examples. At the end of February, however, it was announced that, until the new measures were in operation, wage increases would be rolled back to their average level of the last quarter of 1986, with deduction of any-thing that had been obtained above in the mean time. The pay packets at the beginning of March were so much lighter than those of the previous month that they caused a spate of strikes. Work stoppages in Yugoslavia are neither legal nor illegal. They should not occur, but they do, and they are tolerated. According to official trade union figures, the number of strikes has regularly gone up, from 174 in 1982 to 900 in 1986.

What happened in March 1987 was a veritable workers' revolt, which disrupted industry, and applied to all sectors throughout the country, particularly in Croatia. Some 168 strikes were recorded, affecting more than 20,000 workers. The one at the Labin coal mine in Istria lasted for thirty-four days. The scale of the movement surprised and alarmed the authorities, who backed down. At the end of March, the government amended its legislation on wages by introducing flexible implementation and exemptions. Whole sectors were exempted from the freeze. In July there were 40–70 per cent rises in rents and the cost of electricity, coal, transport, medicines and postal services. In August the price of bread soared by 40–150 per cent. The strikes seemed about to resume or to continue. To placate the workers, temporary price controls were imposed again. A series of products were blocked for three months at their December 1986 prices, and controls on the price of bread were laid down once more forty-eight hours after they had been lifted. For the first time workers had spontaneously downed tools, with the support of trade union leaders, to get the government to backtrack, and they had called for the resignation of the prime minister.

Growing pressure of another kind has been coming from the intelligentsia, and it has been particularly strong in Slovenia and in Serbia. University students and their publications have mocked the cult of Tito and the revolution. In Ljubljana, students came out openly in 1987 against the continued rituals leading up to the annual Day of Youth (Tito's birthday). The poster which was approved for that occasion caused a scandal when it was discovered simply to have been adapted from a Nazi poster of 1936. (It was designed by the Irwin group of painters who, with the Red Pilot theatre and the Laibach rock band, are linked in the so-called '*Neue Slowenische Kunst*' school of young Slovenian artists – arrogant, iconoclastic and hard-currency-earning.)

In May 1985 the Serbian Academy set up a working party to prepare a document on Yugoslavia's social and ethnic issues. Having worked at a slow academic pace, the members of the working party had put together some sort of a preliminary draft in September 1986 which the authorities came to know about. The document challenged the whole system of monopoly of power which, among other things, had weakened Serbia, and it warned that unless liberal reforms were introduced the federal system might fall apart. A war of words started between the government and the Academy – which stuck to its guns, and refused to celebrate its own centenary in 1986. Slovenian intellectuals then came up with their counterpart to the 'memorandum' of the Serbian Academy; that was a special issue of the Ljubljana periodical *Nova revija*. The request that both the contributors to *Nova revija* and the designers of the Day-of-Youth poster should be prosecuted for 'hostile propaganda', under the infamous article 133 of the Penal Code which makes a crime of non-conforming opinions, was actually turned down by the public prosecutor of Slovenia. That, no less than the strikes, was a momentous 'first'.

Founded in Belgrade in 1984, the Committee for the Defence of Freedom of Thought and Expression is virtually an offshoot of the Academy. Made up of leading Serbian writers, artists and scholars, most of whom have been active Communists, with a partisan hero to boot, it records all transgressions to that freedom, meets regularly, and addresses open protests to constitutional institutions, executive, legislative and judicial. Far from being limited to Serbia, it covers the whole state. In particular, it rushed to the support of the Croat Dobroslav Paraga in March 1987.

Back in 1980, Paraga, then a nineteen-year-old practising Catholic student in Zagreb, had collected signatures for a petition demanding an amnesty for political prisoners. In 1981 this earned him a four-year prison term. Then in 1987, after he had described the situation in which political prisoners were held in Yugoslavia, he was then tried again for slandering the state and spreading false information. His new trial mobilised the intelligentsia with appeals from various quarters, including a sensational intervention by the archbishop of Zagreb, Cardinal Kuharić. The result was the relatively mild sentence of six months in prison, suspended but linked with, and followed by, three years of silence. In October 1986, the Belgrade committee also submitted a set of proposals to the Federal Assembly for changes in the existing legislation, to establish the rule of law, along with free and direct elections.

Yet another initiative was launched in Belgrade in December 1986. This was a proposal to set up a Solidarity Fund as a voluntary association to help all those whose livelihood was threatened because of opinions they had expressed, irrespective of their beliefs. The proposal was accompanied by a manifesto denouncing all sectarianisms no less than the monopoly of power, and calling for the democratisation of social life with the strengthening of public opinion. The appeal was signed by more than 600 prominent individuals, among them two former foreign ministers and leading Serbian Communists, the one-time vice-president

of the Republic, General Koča Popović, and the one-time president of
the League of Communists of Serbia, Marko Nikezić. The list also
included 250 journalists, representing the whole range of the media,
including *Komunist*. The launching of the Solidarity Fund provoked a
fierce outburst of words from the authorities, who denounced it as an
anti-Communist opposition movement. Pressure to renege was resisted,
despite some expulsions from the Party. Clearly, the press was slipping
out of control.

In 1985 delegates of the writers' associations from all the republics met
for the first time after ten years. It had been feared that they would disgrace themselves by indulging in sectarian squabbles. It had not been
expected that they would take up a position in favour of the freedom of
culture and creation, and against the expression of opinion being a criminal offence. Throughout 1986 and 1987, several hundred intellectuals
were standing up to be counted, in appeals and petitions calling for
respect for human rights, an end to political monopoly, and the
introduction of democratic reforms. Many of them had been prominent
Communists; some had even been political leaders and partisan generals.
An all-Yugoslav opposition platform, however inchoate, had emerged,
and there was evidence that the mood was spreading to the Party itself.
The failure to grapple with the economic crisis has removed the last
shreds of credibility from the people in charge.

The general crisis of the system has given rise to doubts and a brooding
re-examination of the past; there is a deepening concern that the present
political system cannot survive and hence there is openness to change. In
1987 few people remained who still looked back with nostalgia to the era
of Tito. There was widespread popular agreement with the intellectuals
that the political system was responsible for the economic bankruptcy,
and that change must come – to include the political leadership put
together by Tito in the last decade of his reign.

The opposition platform is not an opposition movement, however. Its
aim is not to win power, but to establish and maintain respect for some
basic values of civilised society. One can actually define its common,
fundamental demands as being: the release of all political prisoners and
the repeal of article 133 of the Penal Code; an end to the intimidation of
individuals and groups struggling for the rule of law, human rights and a
democratic alternative; the public expression and discussion of their
ideas, and the establishment of a dialogue with them; the link-up of
international aid with the respect by the government of its international
undertakings and commitments.

The loss of legitimacy and the pressure for change

Yugoslavia now has an authoritarian, narrow-minded and second-rate leadership. It is so divided among itself, not only on regional lines, that it no longer clearly understands what it is trying to do, beyond preserving its power. However authoritarian, it has to share power with the market; it tries alternately, or simultaneously, to adapt to it and oppose it, and this it does unsuccessfully. The ruling League of Communists is reduced to adapting itself endlessly to circumstances in order to keep its monopoly of political power and the privileges that go with it. These circumstances vary, not only from year to year but from region to region.

It still reacts against anything that could compete with its own ideology – from parliamentary pluralism, which it calls 'right-wing opposition', to spiritual renewal, which it calls 'spiritual counter-revolution' – at a time when its legitimising slogans are all being demystified. It is frightened by the all-Yugoslav character of the pressure for change. Indeed, in March 1987 the partisan veterans' organisation rightly denounced the links between opposition centres in Belgrade, Ljubljana and Zagreb on the question of the 'Third Yugoslavia' – the Yugoslavia of tomorrow.

It resorts to half-baked trials of dissidents, to threats, and to words. Generals have again taken to growling in public that the army could not remain indifferent to all the shameful things being done by workers, students, intellectuals, historians, publishers and journalists. Taking pride of place was the interview given to *Der Spiegel* in March 1987 by the prime minister, Branko Mikulić, on the eve of his visit to West Germany, when he denounced all the opposition as being not only reactionary, but linked to reactionary centres abroad that wanted to destabilise Yugoslavia, branded Djilas as a traitor *'par excellence'*, and warned that 'we shall defend our system by all available means, including the army'.

The rest was words. There was little else at the Thirteenth Party Congress held in June 1986. It was so uninteresting that it could only be enlivened by 'fringe' events. Jovanka Broz, who had been Tito's estranged wife, came to the Congress, and had to be expelled by the police. An old man climbed up a tree, and kept shouting that the Party had reduced the country to the wretched state it was in. The police could not get him down, and had to call the fire brigade. Since the Twelfth Congress, Party membership had fallen by 140,000; workers make up only 30 per cent current membership. Yet in the spring of 1987, the Central Committee still issued threats against those favouring an alternative system of liberal democracy, before acknowledging plainly in the summer that the problem was . . . that Party policy was not being implemented. No wonder that a Belgrade lawyer wanted to sue the League of Communists for not having fulfilled its promises, and force it to return all the Party subscriptions he had paid since joining in 1962.

The leadership had decided in principle, in 1985, to try and overcome existing constitutional obstacles to the further development of a market economy, and to extend federal powers over economic affairs. It took a while to obtain the necessary consensus on a scheme, which was finally submitted in February 1987. Limited to vague proposals for better legal guarantees to private small enterprises, for rationalised planning as a way of working towards an integrated Yugoslav market, and for a unified tax system, it fell short of radical change. In the mind of public opinion, the proposals confirmed that the system had exhausted its resources and could not deal with the situation, and hence that the country faced the collapse of living standards and the likelihood of a deeper political crisis.

At a popular level, the legitimacy of the Communist Party had resided essentially in the following achievements: it had ended the civil war and brought the various ethnic groups out of their blind alleys; it had then stood up to Stalin and Soviet Russia; finally, it had introduced the Yugoslavs to the joys of consumerism, and it had put the country on the map. All that was now finished or meaningless. While the Party realised it had lost its credibility, it still clung to its interpretation of the war, which seemed to be its only remaining source of legitimacy. The political establishment likes to think that the People's Liberation Movement has made an important contribution to history. It is still obsessed with Yugoslavia having been a major factor in bringing about the defeat of Nazi-Fascism. The number of ex-partisans continues to grow (whereas officially there were 800,000 of them when the war ended, in 1983 there were one million members of the League of Associations of Combatants of the People's Liberation Army). And the government still looks around for ancient war criminals among its fascist and not-so-fascist opponents of the time.

While Spain united on the fiftieth anniversary of the beginning of her civil war in saying that a fratricidal war was not an event to celebrate, that it now belonged to history, and 'never again', Yugoslavia instead celebrated her participation in the Spanish Civil War. Any suggestion that Yugoslavia had generally been no more than a side-show during the

1939–45 war, albeit a relatively important one from time to time, was
deemed unpatriotic and reactionary. The same was said of the trend that
was beginning to consider what had happened during the tragic years in
Yugoslavia as being more important than the country's actual contribution to victory.

Yugoslavia is but one instance of the general East European tension
between the societies and the regimes that govern them. The regimes all
face the same dilemma – how to modernise the economy without changing the distribution of power. Those in government who want to
'modernise' do not necessarily want to 'liberalise' or 'democratise'.
What they advocate when they use such words is the minimum of freedom required to obtain greater efficiency. When obliged to choose
between pressing ahead with modernisation and keeping their grip on
policy, they are liable to see the case for putting the second of these alternatives ahead of the first. Most Communist leaderships are anyway too
divided to come to terms with the question of how to modernise the
economy without modernising politics, and they end up with a hopeless
confusion of carrots and sticks.

Over the years, they had become less dependent on day-to-day repression, and more on consumerism, to sustain their legitimacy. In so doing
they had become hostages to continued economic development, for
which a vital pre-condition was structural reform – deemed incompatible with the 'leading role of the Party'. Many tried to develop economic ties with the West as a way of sustaining growth, or of expanding
their independence from Moscow, or both, without fundamental
reforms. They were willing to risk subversive Western influences coming in with economic contacts, calculating that they would be
neutralised by the consumer satisfaction of material gains. The Western
connection thus usually coincided with the weakening of the reform
movement. It worked until the end of the 1970s, when the connection
also meant that such economies were not protected from the rise in
energy prices and the recession. In the early 1980s, all East European systems (with the possible exception of Albania, whose leadership had not
become hostage to economic progress) thus came under increasing challenge from within.

Yugoslavia's difference is that it pioneered all these attempts and
dilemmas, out of necessity. From the 1960s, through consumerism, freedom of movement and corruption, her rulers had given the average citi-
zen an *ersatz* version of liberty. In the 1980s, when all East European
regimes are desperately trying to re-legitimise themselves, there are few

rewards for Yugoslavia in having already tried it all. As elsewhere in Eastern Europe, so too in Yugoslavia the legitimacy of the regime has no firmer foundation than the takeover of power by a minority group, albeit supported by a patriotic movement, and the continuity of the leadership has been all-important.

To many people today in the West, Yugoslavia appears more and more as a country riddled with debt and financial scandals, ethnically divided and unstable, whose problems cannot be solved by the inefficient leadership in Belgrade and in the regional capitals. And yet for decades – in fact at least up till the demission of Titoism – we were told that Titoist Yugoslavia was a good thing. The Western resolve to sustain Communist rule there rested on the belief that only Tito's Party could keep the country out of Soviet control and united.

The Communists did emerge from the intercommunal atrocities of the war as unifiers of sorts. However, it should be remembered that there had been no physical clashes between Yugoslav ethnic groups as such before the Axis got down to exploiting their differences shamelessly in the course of the Second World War. Even then, those who were not ideologically committed to the Axis, or directly in its service continued to pay at least lip-service to the ideal and concept of a united Yugoslavia; and before the war, there had been active co-operation between the political parties of the various national communities in trying to restore parliamentary government in order to set Yugoslavia on a new course.

To acquire a monopoly of power and then preserve it has been the first task of the Yugoslav Communist leadership. This was true in the initial period, when Tito was anticipating and fomenting revolution outside his country's borders, while at the same time fearing the victory of anti-Communist forces within them. This was true in the middle period, when he handled the nationalities issue according to the divide-and-rule principle which came to accentuate the cleavages between the component nations and regions. It was also true in the final period, when he delegated power to his trusties in the republics who in the intervening years have drawn first on nationalistic feelings and then on international credit, to build up their own separate power bases.

Before they came to power, Yugoslavia's Communists followed the Leninist idea of a revolutionary party which would be firm in its ideology and organisation, but ready to make concessions and tactical alliances, and prepared to take popular ideas and slogans over from their opponents. They were internationalists, but they were not above using conflicts among nationalities. They distinguished between the nationalism of the oppressed, which they supported, and that of the oppressors, which they opposed. Having come to power, they settled the nationalities issue on paper. In practice, they tried to rein in and weaken the two main ones, the Serbian and the Croatian; they exaggerated the role of the new yet genuine Macedonian identity, and they allowed free scope to the older but more questionable Montenegrin identity. When nationalism developed within their own ranks and as a consequence of their own policies, beyond acceptable limits, they called it 'counter-revolutionary'. Eventually, they were to exacerbate the issue to the point where the ethnic components of Yugoslavia are coming to lose any feeling for their common destiny and even for their common interests.

Tito endorsed the concept of self-management as a public-relations exercise to rehabilitate Yugoslavia within the 'socialist' movement. After going through various hesitant phases, it ended up as a charade of workers' participation, effectively controlled by political coteries. The experience has revealed the fictitious character of self-management where a Leninist party keeps the monopoly of political power. Under this system, Yugoslavia was living well beyond her means by the time of Tito's death, foreign credits making up the difference. Decades of irresponsible political investment and management now demand the adoption of drastic measures, in an atmosphere of high inflation, falling standards of living, financial scandals involving the political leadership, and rising discontent, the victims being the working people on whose behalf the system was invented.

The cult of Tito was one of the elements used by the Yugoslav leadership to maintain continuity, and to profit from his prestige in the East where he was known and esteemed, in the West where he was less known and more admired, and among the non-aligned to whom he had extended help and a certain significance in world affairs. In the few years immediately following on his death, the cult even grew to unbelievable proportions – inspired, again unwittingly, by a pseudo-Christian conception of life after death, with echoes of the real presence, the incarnation and the transfiguration – before the myth shrank back to the dimensions of reality. Now that the leaders must at last face up to the tensions and problems that assail the system, it is seen that Tito and his cult, while containing them, had also prevented the quest for practical solutions. In an atmosphere where the legend loses every day more of its consistency, taboos are being lifted all the time.

How far can change be implemented without losing the monopoly of power of the League of Communists? How can the monopoly be maintained without a military-backed solution in a society so obviously diverse? How can the development and consolidation of a new bourgeoisie be held back without a Mao-type cultural revolution? How can the citizens, now that they have tasted the joys of consumerism, be prevented from wanting to choose political as well as economic goods without a drastic revision of the theoretical foundations of self-management? How can one defend the independence of Yugoslavia, placed by geography at a dangerous crossroads, but one which is nevertheless once again well in Europe, without mooring her somewhere? These are some of the important questions that Tito's heirs are being faced with.

They are being assailed by them at a time when ideologies generally, and Marxism-Leninism more particularly, have lost their attraction, and when the prolonged economic crisis has led to a total loss of confidence in slogans. Pressure for change in Yugoslavia is coming from below, and it is pressure for political change. 'In times of austerity, politics is at least something a poor country can afford. Ten years is a long deprivation.' So wrote a leading article in the London *Times* on Chile under 'Poor Old Pinochet' on the tenth anniversary of the coup that installed him in power. Something similar could be said of Yugoslavia after 'poor old Tito', unless it were considered that her many decades of deprivation made politics something that she could never afford again. A growing section of Yugoslav public opinion aspires to a political evolution towards more pluralism, more legality, more accountability, more rationality, more reality. Its educated élite clamours for it.

The bond that Yugoslavs most need, at the time when the country enters the eighth decade of its existence, is the bond of respect for each other's beliefs, opinions and traditions. Those in authority not unnaturally still fail to understand that policy conflicts are a normal facet of democracy. Both government and opposition need to accept open debate on all important problems – a responsible debate, without dogmatism or exclusivism. While the government should accept that irrational fears about the survival of a nation as a unique entity are a powerful motor, intellectual élites are beginning to recognise that passionate expressions of grief, mutual recriminations and sectarian incidents are no way to advance the interests of their respective communities. The sooner the opening-up process begins, to involve all those who believe in non-violent change, the better, for the ultimate answers to Yugoslavia's problems can only result from an interaction of those different points of view.

The process can only be initiated within the ruling party, for there is no other organized political or social force in the country. The regime already knows a broad range of implementation of its model, from Bosnia-Herzegovina at its most closed to Slovenia at its most open. If the Party turned its eyes away from that bastion of neo-Stalinism that is the central republic, and looked to the northern one for inspiration, it would see that the local government in Ljubljana already functions with a degree of openness that accepts criticism, and that it is increasingly prepared to take the public into its confidence through informal consultations, to establish popular responses to Party initiatives. That there has been no collapse into anarchy in Slovenia is evidence that such an evolution need not mean the end of the existing order based on socialism and non-alignment. Serbian opinion holds the balance. It could force the regime to open up, behave responsibly, and take the citizens into its confidence, or it could rally to a hard-line course which would allegedly save the common state by restoring order and curbing disruptive separatists.

Yugoslavia at seventy

As we have pointed out, Yugoslavia does exist, without a perceptible alternative. She has a prehistory of common influences, common moulds and common mentalities which gave birth to a Yugoslav idea and a Yugoslav movement before these eventually led to the formation of the Yugoslav state. And since 1918 Yugoslavia has survived, however improbably. She has, in fact, survived in spite of the problems and the crises. She has been destroyed, and has come together again.

Both in 1918 and in 1945, there was no real alternative to a Yugoslav solution, but the citizens of Yugoslavia were never actually and directly consulted. Self-determination has somehow been exercised through solutions implemented by a relative majority, or by force of arms and circumstances or by unsatisfactory compromises with the rulers. The state has been identified with the rulers, and, even though there has never been a military dictatorship, the army has always been considered as the ultimate and conservative defender of the constitutional order. Rarely has there been a real compromise between Yugoslavia's component groups, ethnic or political, preceded by a real debate; rarely have any means of promoting integration been allowed, let alone encouraged, other than those of the current official ideology.

The history of Yugoslavia is littered with missed opportunities, from the unification of 1918 to the groundswell of 1968 fifty years later, by

way of Davidović's cabinet of 1924, the electoral success of the United
Opposition in 1938, and the break with Stalin in 1948. The self-
determination of Yugoslavia's nations should be exercised formally, if
only for psychological reasons – for the Serbs to be freed from the complex of having imposed unification, and the non-Serbs to be rid of theirs
of having had unification imposed on them. A country cannot, after all,
be permanently in search of its birth certificate.

But is Yugoslavia worth keeping? Why should it be kept united at all
costs? Because the Powers consider it advantageous? Because the Yugoslavs find it to their benefit? Because there is no way of separating them?
Population transfers are always painful. They can be more or less
ordered, when imposed through a peace settlement by the winners on
the losers. They are chaotic, when states divide or disintegrate. Nevertheless, they are a radical way of separating populations when all rational
arguments in favour of unity no longer carry weight. All the same, if
that were to happen in Yugoslavia, the very scale of all the dimensions of
the operation (in terms of territory, population and international consequences) would dwarf the sad events of Cyprus and Lebanon. The
principle by which the Yugoslav community is judged must eventually
be the exercise of reason through the freedom of action of its nationalities
and citizens. Until the time comes when this is obtained, its ongoing
national question will remain a permanent temptation for the mischief-
makers of intransigent one-sided solutions that do not solve anything in
the long run, and for those who fish in troubled international waters. A
grand 'Lebanonisation' of Yugoslavia, as a 'worst case', cannot be
excluded.

It seems at least probable that a majority of Yugoslavs accept the need
to live in the political community of a Yugoslav state, and that they even
go along with the general framework of the existing system for as long as
it functions more or less adequately to generate economic advance, and to
overcome the fear of the unknown. But would a programme that offered
nothing more specific, more positive and more attractive suffice to prevent irrational leaps into the dark, if the economy continued to deteriorate and the system no longer functioned?

Serbs and Croats are condemned by history, geography and language
either to live together or to eliminate each other. To the north, Slovenia
feels that her economy is subsidising an inefficient economic system, an
inept political machinery, and a misdirected development strategy. In
May 1987 the average wage in Slovenia was 219,758 dinars, compared to
95,526 in Kosovo, with Croatia (147,004), inner Serbia (125,217),

Voivodina (122,689), Bosnia and Herzegovina (118,040), Montenegro (103,930) and Macedonia (98,807) in between. Macedonia, to the south, still needs subsidies for her bankrupt economy, and support from a political system that has acknowledged her existence. However, there is at present no real separatist tendency, let alone a separatist movement, among the South Slav nations of Yugoslavia. (The Albanians of Yugoslavia, who live in three republics – southern Serbia, western Macedonia and eastern Montenegro, in proximity to the Republic of Albania – and account for a third of the total number of Albanians, are a different, if all-important, problem.) Not a single one of them is, by itself, strong enough to break up the community, and most of them would not survive well on their own. For the time being, the regional particularisms and their various attitudes towards the common state are a factor of diversification and hence an agent tending to dissolve the political authoritarianism   that has aggravated the nationalities issue but still claims to possess the only key to it.

If the Yugoslavs are to continue living together in a united country, and if that country is not to become again the proverbial powder-keg that starts off European crises, it is essential that they should be able to participate fully in the development of their community. They must be able to appreciate its deeper advantages, to reflect on what put them on the path to unification before the First World War, and what made them kill each other and yet remain united during and after the Second World War. They must be able to express their different ways of thinking otherwise than by hurling themselves into sectarian impasses, and they must know what is implied by cohabitation and by divorce. They have not had a democratic government since 1929. Since 1980 they have no longer had a 'king', but they will need a period of transition before they can decide on any constitutional change – a period of transition when freedom of movement, freedom of expression and freedom of association would be fully guaranteed.

Change must come from inside Yugoslavia, but the West could give change a chance to occur. The West cannot be indifferent to the plight of an autocratic oligarchical regime trying to find its way to a measure of freedom and democracy. Yugoslavia is too near to the European Community for its member-states to watch indifferently what is happening there – as Italian commentators are apt to point out. The West should no longer be seen to be backing a government against the advocates of the rule of law, for the sake of 'stability' and 'independence', and without considering that it could thereby destabilise public morale and national unity to the point where foreign interference was facilitated rather than warded off. Support for a manifestly incompetent and unaccountable government, alienated from public opinion at home, for the sake of keeping the Russians at bay, as in the days of the Cold War, or as in Palmerston's days, is superannuated.

It would be more imaginative now to think of encouraging those who are looking for a more pluralistic if less anti-Soviet regime. Most Communists would favour change, but they do not really know what sort of change, and are confused. The ruling minority holds on to power, and does not know what to do with it. There is nothing wrong with trying to identify trends within the ruling party, to embolden those who want the system to evolve, to give moral support to people who have the courage to stand up for intellectual and spiritual freedom, and to politicians who seem ready to grapple with problems that are a threat to the situation in Europe. Western enthusiasm with, and lack of understanding for, regimes considered stable or safe has often been misguided, and can contribute to their tragic end. There is no need to worry so much about a bit of destabilisation that would encourage those who want to open out towards political democracy and economic liberalisation, and give Yugoslavia a chance to grope towards some broadly-based and accepted stability.

SUGGESTIONS FOR FURTHER READING

There is no short history of Yugoslavia that can be recommended, not even in the Cambridge University Press series which offers excellent volumes on modern Greece (by Richard Clogg, 2nd edn 1986) and on modern Bulgaria (by R.J. Crampton, 1987). Both of these throw indirect light on the history of Yugoslavia. Otherwise, and more directly, the reader will still have to go to the present author's pioneering *Yugoslavia* in the 'Nations of the Modern World' series (Benn, London, and Praeger, New York, 1971). *The Creation of Yugoslavia, 1914–1918*, edited by Dimitrije Djordjević (Clio Books, Santa Barbara and Oxford, 1980), is a mixed collection of conference papers, with an excellent introductory chapter by Djordjević himself ('The Idea of Yugoslav Unity in the Nineteenth Century'). Ivo Banac, *The National Question in Yugoslavia* (Cornell University Press, Ithaca and London, 1984) is important, erudite, one-sided, emotional, prejudiced and disappointing. Djordjević goes on to look at 'Three Yugoslavias – A Case for Survival', in his 1984 lecture to the American Historical Association as chairman of the US Conference on Slavic and East European History (*East European Quarterly*, XIX/4, 1986).

Phyllis Auty, *Tito* (Longman, London, 1970) piles on the admiration felt in the 1960s, while Nora Beloff, *Tito's Legacy* (Gollancz, London, 1985) does her best to expose the myth in the 1980s. The reader should then turn to Milovan Djilas, *Tito – The Story from Inside* (Weidenfeld and Nicolson, London, 1981).

Dennison Rusinow, *The Yugoslav Experiment, 1948–1974* (C. Hurst & Co., London, 1977); Dusan Doder, *The Yugoslavs* (Random House, New York, 1978, and Allen and Unwin, London, 1979); and K. Krishna Moorthy, *After Tito What?* (Humanities Press, Atlantic Highlands, N.J., 1980) cover, in their different ways, Yugoslavia from the late 1940s to the late 1970s. On religion, Stella Alexander, *Church and State in Yugoslavia since 1945* (Cambridge University Press, Cambridge, 1979) is a useful chronicle.

INDEX

Adriatic Sea, 4, 11, 13, 80–1, 112, 121
Afghanistan, 43, 112, 120
Africa, 114, 116, 121
agrarian reform, 5, 67
Albania: 4, 24, 66, 71, 74, 78–93
passim, 118, 121, 150, 156;
Albanian minority in Yugoslavia,
29, 66–7, 71–2, 74, 78–93, passim,
107, 118, 156; Albanian nationa-
lism, 74, 80, 87, 93, 108
Alexander, King, 1, 3–4, 6, 52, 54,
58–9, 68–9, 100
Algeria, 93, 114–15
Allied powers (in Second World
War), 8, 11–14, 17, 38–40, 113
Amnesty International, 33
Angola, 119
Ankara, 121, 127
Anti-Fascist Council for the National
Liberation of Yugoslavia, v, 16
Antonescu, Marshal, 40
Arabs, 114–16
Armed forces: of Serbia, 62; of pre-
war Yugoslavia, 41, 62; of post-
war Yugoslavia, 26, 44, 61–2,
122–3, 148
Athenagoras, Patriarch, 104
Athens, 117–18, 121, 127
Austria: 6, 16–17, 123; Yugoslav
minority in, 17
Austria-Hungary, see Habsburg
Monarchy
Axis, vi, 8, 10–12, 15, 37–8, 46, 53,
70, 82, 101, 113, 139–40, 151

Baghdad, 121
Balkan co-operation, 117–18, 126–7
Balkan Entente, 6
Balkan federation, 17, 71

Balkan Pact, 113
Balkan Wars, 2, 61–2, 67, 80–1 ·
Balkans, 9, 12–13, 67, 76, 78–9, 90,
94–6, 118, 127–8
Bárre, Raymond, 35
Belgrade: 13–14, 32, 39, 52, 57–8,
71–3, 75–6, 86, 88–9, 91–3,
114–5, 127, 129, 132, 135–6, 139,
141, 143, 146, 148, 151;
conference of non-aligned states,
20, 115; University, 84, 136, 139
Beloff, Nora, 33
Berlin, Congress of, 66, 80
Bettiza, Enzo, 51
Biber, Dušan, 139
Bilandžić, Dušan, 34
Bitola, 80
Bogumils, 95
Borba, 31
Bosnia and Herzegovina, 10–11, 29,
39, 66, 70, 83, 95, 98, 101, 107–8,
131, 154, 158
Brazil, 28
Brezhnev, Leonid, 22–3, 42
Britain, see Great Britain
Broz, Josip, see Tito
Broz, Jovanka, 148
Budapest, 96, 98
Bulganin, Marshal, 19
Bulgaria: 71, 77, 89, 103, 105, 117,
123, 127; Turkish minority in, 121
Bulgars, 64, 67
Byzantine Empire, 94–5

Cairo, 115
Carlowitz, see Sremski Karlovci
Catholic Church, 10–11, 59, 65–6,
76, 80, 94–110 passim, 146
Čavoški, Kosta, 135
Chamberlain, Neville, 51

161

164   *Index*